Navan Fort
Archaeology and Myth

Chris Lynn

Navan Fort
Archaeology and Myth

Chris Lynn

Wordwell

ENVIRONMENT
AND HERITAGE
SERVICE

First published in 2003
Wordwell Ltd
PO Box 69, Bray, Co. Wicklow

Published under licence for the Environment and Heritage Service, an executive agency of the Department of the Environment (Northern Ireland).

Applications for reproduction should be made in writing to:

Environment and Heritage Service, Built Heritage, Waterman House, 5–33 Hill Street, Belfast BT1 2LA.

ISBN 1 869857 67 4

British Library Cataloguing-in-Publication Data.
A catalogue record for this book is available from the British Library.

Cover design: Rachel Dunne
Editor: Aisling Flood
Typeset by Wordwell Ltd
Printed in Spain by E.G. Zure

Contents

Figures

used to convert the Navan samples into methane.

Fig. 26: Burnt soil and charcoal in one of the Navan Fort ring-slots (Site A, Slot A2).

Fig. 27: Plans of the Iron Age figure-of-eight structures at Navan and Knockaulin, Co. Kildare.

Fig. 28: 'Rose' phase structure at Knockaulin interpreted as an unroofed arena.

Fig. 29: Skull of a Barbary ape from the Iron Age layers under the Navan mound (photo: British Museum).

Fig. 30: Aerial view of the King's Stables, a pool surrounded by a bank covered with trees (photo: Mick Aston).

Fig. 31: Beginning the dig in the waterlogged interior of the King's Stables.

Fig. 32: Facial part of a human skull found in the bottom of the King's Stables pool.

Fig. 33: Plan of the Dorsey based on H.G. Tempest's study.

Fig. 34: Map showing sections of 'linear earthworks' in the north of Ireland.

Fig. 35: Gully and burnt material found under the bank of the Dorsey on the north-east (north is to the left).

Fig. 36: Oak post-bases and side-pieces uncovered at the western end of the Dorsey in 1977.

Fig. 37: Diagram showing how tree-ring patterns can be matched backwards from the present.

Fig. 38: The quarry and industrial site between Navan, centre left, and Loughnashade, right, looking west.

Fig. 39: Haughey's Fort from the south, showing the excavation trench in the centre and an outer ditch as a cropmark in the field to the north (photo: Queen's University, Belfast).

Fig. 40: Concentric arcs of post- and stake-holes at the centre of Haughey's Fort (photo: Queen's University, Belfast).

Fig. 41: Excavated stretch of the inner ditch of Haughey's Fort on the south-east (photo: Queen's University, Belfast).

Fig. 42: Cup-and-ring marked stone uncovered in Haughey's Fort (photo: Queen's University, Belfast).

Fig. 43: Bronze disc decorated in La Tène style forming the bell end of the horn from Loughnashade, first century BC/AD (photo: National Museum of Ireland).

Fig. 44: The Navan area from the air looking north. Navan Fort and Loughnashade are on the right; Haughey's Fort and the King's Stables are to the left.

Fig. 45: Iron Age 'safety-pin' brooch found near Navan. The central setting probably contained enamel (photo: National Museum of Ireland).

Fig. 46: Brooch found near Navan Fort, fifth century AD (photo: Ulster Museum).

Fig. 47: Map of Armagh by Richard Bartlett made in 1601 showing Navan at the top (west) skirted by the old road running east across the River Callan to Armagh (National Library of Ireland).

Fig. 48: Aerial view of Navan Centre from the west; carpark right, buildings centre left (photo: Mick Aston).

Preface

Navan Fort, Co. Armagh, is owned by the Department of the Environment and is managed by the Environment and Heritage Service. At intervals over a period of some 40 years the staff of the Department have carried out, collaborated in and sponsored archaeological survey, excavation and research into this famous site and the monuments in the surrounding landscape. This book is an attempt to provide a straightforward summary of that work and includes an account of one of the most interesting and intriguing archaeological excavations carried out in Ireland. The site of the legendary and 'far-famed' Emain Macha (now known as Navan Fort) has been known from before the beginning of Irish history. There is a possibility that some of the legends associated with it have come down to us from a time when such myths were a part of everyday life and religion. Navan is not a site like Troy or Knossos that was lost and had to be rediscovered. In the myths and legends of the Ulaidh (the 'Ulstermen') Emain is portrayed as a royal headquarters, the capital of a warlike aristocracy and a place of assembly for the people occupying the northern quarter of Ireland.

Irish legend identifies a number of places as regional centres of importance or as provincial royal capitals. Most of the sites identified in legend as ancient centres have complexes of unusual earthwork monuments, which also underline the significance of the places. But the Early Christian and medieval scribes who wrote down the tales were not consciously constructing links between places that had groups of strange monuments and the literary tradition. Some of the places mentioned in the tales are now unknown, and there are impressive monumental sites that find no mention in the literary tradition. Besides Navan Fort in Ulster, the places celebrated in ancient lore as provincial centres include Cruachan in Connacht, Dún Ailinne in Leinster and Tara in County Meath.

Some digging was carried out in Tara by the British-Israelites at the end of the nineteenth century. Scientific excavations were carried out there by S.P. Ó Ríordáin and Ruaidhrí de Valera in the 1950s. These proved that one of the monuments at the site (the 'Mound of the Hostages') was a passage tomb of the Neolithic period, dating from around 3500–2900 BC. Another site excavated was the 'Rath of the Synods'. This earthwork proved to have had a long sequence of development culminating in a fort or rath surrounded by several roughly circular banks. Scattered finds of Roman material suggested that there had been activity there in the early centuries of the first millennium AD. No other excavation was carried out on the monuments of legendary fame until the Ministry of Finance began excavation in Navan Fort in connection with the Archaeological Survey of County Armagh in 1961. The excavations continued through the 1960s on a large artificial mound that dominated the centre of the monument. The mound proved to be something never seen before or since in an archaeological excavation. The remains of a huge circular wooden building constructed shortly after 100 BC had been carefully enshrined inside it. I was privileged as a student to assist in the later stages of the excavation.

This book attempts to tell the story of the excavation and more recent discoveries in the area in a form that is hopefully more engaging than the official report on the excavation. It is a personal account, coloured by first-hand experience, and is told in a matter-of-fact way, refraining from creation of atmosphere and dramatic tension, in the hope that the significance of the rapid series of discoveries leading to unexpected conclusions will keep interest alive. The reader is advised, however, that opinion is divided on the interpretation of some aspects of the site and the excavation. Navan Fort is often said to be Northern Ireland's most significant prehistoric site and is claimed as the capital of an ancient kingdom, the territory of a ruling dynasty that had been overthrown before history began in the seventh century AD. The excavation and fieldwork that have taken place over the last 40 years enable debate on the date and purpose of the monument to be expanded in the light of fuller knowledge.

C.L.
October 2003

Acknowledgements

Many people who contributed in various ways to Navan-related research are acknowledged in the text. Here I would like to thank those who had a hand in the production of the book: Gail Pollock and Mark Mulholland of the Photographic and Design Unit, Built Heritage, Environment and Heritage Service (EHS), for preparation of the illustrations and work on the layout; Deiri Warner and Gillian Gilmore for preparing line drawings at short notice; Jim and Conall Mallory for reading and making suggestions on the draft text; the staff of Wordwell, in particular Aisling Flood, for checking text, making helpful suggestions and seeing the work through press; Bernard Moane and Ronnie Morrison of the EHS for helping me make the time to get the work finished; and Nuala Lynn, for encouragement and understanding as I brought the work to a conclusion. I am also grateful to the members of the Navan Research Group, Mike Baillie, Barrie Hartwell, Jim Mallory, Richard Warner and Dave Weir, and other contributors to the journal *Emania* for providing rich sources of inspiration.

Introduction

Usually, to save time and confusion, archaeological reports on excavations summarise everything that is known about a site at the time of writing and describe its excavated features in chronological order, oldest first. Such a report would summarise the evidence for human activity on the site beginning in earliest times and, working toward the present, would discuss the latest interpretation of the discoveries. This book, however, takes a more historical approach and attempts to describe the sequence of discoveries at the site in the order in which they occurred. For example, in the case of the major excavation on the main mound in Navan, we will go from the top down, in the original sequence of excavation. In describing the earlier research, I will not anticipate insights gained as a result of more recent excavations. Rather, the story of the investigations themselves will be allowed to unfold as it happened, in order to communicate something of the ongoing excitement of the succession of new discoveries and insights.

I first encountered Navan Fort in the mid-1950s when I was taken on outings with the Armagh Field Club. I recall the enthusiasm for the site of T.G.F. Paterson, curator of Armagh County Museum, and F.J. Hughes, chair of the Diocesan Historical Society (Fig. 1). Their discussions left me with the confident impression that Navan Fort was a fascinating archaeological site, taking its rightful place along with the historical and ecclesiastical wonders of Armagh City and district. While views on what the site was or represented were at an elementary stage of development (for example, the burial site of Queen Macha was suggested), there was local belief in the historical accuracy of the traditions associated with the place.

Fig. 1—F.J. Hughes and T.G.F Paterson at the mound in Navan, c. 1960.

It was seen as the pagan predecessor of the Christian City of Armagh, giving the locality a continuous religious pre-eminence, stretching back into the mists of prehistory.

While I was still at school in Armagh in 1963, awareness was raised in the city by the arrival of a team of American archaeologists to carry out excavations in Navan Fort. While I knew little about what they were doing and had not to my knowledge seen an 'American' in the flesh before, it seemed entirely natural, even in those days, that people with good judgement and the appropriate resources should travel halfway round the world to investigate this monument. The 1963 excavation is where the main story of modern research into Navan Fort and speculation on its purpose begins.

In those days of the mid-1960s the two archaeologists working in the state sector for the Ministry of Finance, D.M. Waterman and A.E.P. (Pat) Collins, shared premises in a terrace of large houses at no. 17 of the tree-lined University Square, Belfast, with the Department of Archaeology. At that time, the job of 'the Ministry' archaeologists was to carry out and publish an archaeological survey of Northern Ireland and to direct associated small-scale research excavations. They had an official brass plate on the front door proclaiming the presence of the 'Archaeological Survey of Northern Ireland'. The sharing of premises arose from the common origin and interests of both groups, in many ways the creations of Professor E.E. Evans, and from an enormous overlap in research projects, shared scientific facilities, the University Library and teaching.

In coming and going to lectures, one sometimes encountered the Ministry archaeologists in the hall and stairs of no. 17. Pat Collins with his long beard was well known around Queen's as the typical archaeologist. His office was readily accessible on the ground floor, and he delighted in helping students, particularly in explaining how to recognise and draw different forms of flint artefacts, but would often digress to explain how to live off the land and to survive in a tent while on excavation. The tall figure of Dudley Waterman could be glimpsed sometimes, pipe in mouth, working energetically in his office on the first floor at a large drawing board.

It was, of course, generally known during my period as an undergraduate that Waterman was directing large-scale and complex excavations of prehistoric structures in Navan Fort, assisted during a two-month summer season by Stephen Rees-Jones, the conservator in the Department of Archaeology, Queen's University. Pat Collins visited the site to take his exemplary photos, using an antiquated-looking but effective plate camera, some of which are reproduced in this book. There was no student participation in the dig and little hard information about what was being uncovered by Waterman and his core team of trusted local workmen who were re-hired every summer for the dig. Public relations were relatively undeveloped in archaeological circles in the 1960s, and visitors were excluded from the excavations for fear of accidental damage to unrecorded features exposed in the soft sandy soil.

I first saw the Navan excavations one evening in 1967 when the site was deserted, and it looked incredibly complicated. At that time I thought that the unexcavated straight-line sections of soil running neatly through the excavated area were the walls of ancient buildings; all the other dug-out features, to the inexperienced eye, looked too complicated and formless to interpret as anything significant. Later, in July that year, during a short break in the training excavation at Ballynagilly, Co. Tyrone, I went with another student, Steve Briggs, to visit the Navan excavations. On climbing the hill, we introduced ourselves at the site; we were told that we could find Waterman in the excavation compound but were advised that he was upset by damage to the site. We introduced ourselves and explained that we were students working at Ballynagilly and that we hoped to become field archaeologists. Waterman questioned the wisdom of this ambition in robust terms.

It transpired that the previous night the wind had blown the plastic covering off the excavated area and a downpour had washed away a series of significant features before they had been photographed and recorded to Waterman's satisfaction. The impact of the problem was lost on us, not having seen the features before the damage, but we realised that running a major excavation would not always be plain sailing. After a few minutes Dudley got up, lit his pipe and showed us what he had found. He soon relaxed and was deep into the story of the excavation, most of it over our heads. At the end of an hour of careful explanation we were deeply impressed by the complexity and interest of the prehistoric structures being uncovered under the mound. The principal impression was of the skill and dedication being applied to the work, from the care and quality of the dig through to the quality of its study and recording. We still, however, had only the vaguest idea of what was being uncovered; the fragile remains of foundation trenches for circular wooden walls and deep pits that had been dug in the centuries immediately before the time of Christ to support strange large wooden structures were unlike anything ever found before (Fig. 2).

Waterman had found evidence in the form of a decorated bronze pin that the site may date from the Early Iron Age, sometime after *c.* 300 BC. This is a period of particular interest and mystery, since it immediately precedes the historic era. It is regarded as the time when much of the culture and polity of early historic Ireland developed, and yet we know relatively little about it. The legendary reputation of the site and the unusual, possibly ceremonial, structures being uncovered lent the place an almost eerie aura and an intense interest. Gradually the idea developed that I might get a chance to work on the site and learn from the latest excavation techniques being applied there. This ambition was realised when, with the help of Roger Weatherup of Armagh County Museum, I managed to get a job in the Navan excavation as an assistant in 1969 and 1970, beginning nearly a decade of inspiring professional involvement with Dudley Waterman and Pat Collins.

It is worth noting that the problem of heavy rain falling on soft soil prompted Waterman to have a large shelter, some 10m by 12m, made the following winter for use on the site in future seasons. The metal framework of the shelter was bolted together in sections, and a small team erected it at the beginning of each season. It had guttering, and its covering could easily be rolled away on fine days.[*]

---

[*]The bolted metal roof-frame of the shelter gives service to this day, covering workshops in the Department of the Environment Historic Monuments Depot in Moira, Co. Down!

Fig. 2—Wall-slots and post-pits in the pre-mound surface.

Chapter 1

Beginning the Navan excavation:
Site A

Navan Fort lies some 2.6km due west of the City of Armagh and some 15km south of Lough Neagh. It is 40km from the sea at Carlingford Lough and is 75m above sea level (Fig. 3). The rich green countryside is of pleasant rolling drumlins (small hills of glacial origin), overlying limestone. The drumlins lie in a wide belt between the uplands of southern and eastern County Armagh and the flat marshy land to the south of Lough Neagh. The River Callan flows northward 2km to the east, and the River Blackwater forms the boundary between counties Armagh and Tyrone 8km to the west. The area is favoured by good soils and a slightly warmer and drier climate than neighbouring areas.

Navan Fort does not occupy a particularly commanding position, and only from the south can its situation in the landscape be appreciated from a distance. The site is usually glimpsed for the first time beside a minor road, 'Navan Fort Road', which follows the line of an ancient routeway running westward from Armagh. The site is referred to locally as a 'fort', and this descriptive term is used on maps. But the site is not a fort in the sense of a military stronghold. The monument is more likely to be a prehistoric sanctuary or enclosed sacred space. It consists of a circular earthwork—a curving bank with an accompanying ditch uphill—250m in diameter (Fig. 4). This layout is unusual because defensive works always have the ditch outside the bank (downhill), giving assailants a long, steep climb while at the mercy of defenders. The earthwork encloses the summit of the drumlin but is not centred on it. One of the reasons for choosing to build the monument here may be that the top of this particular hill is relatively flat and falls away gently to the north and east, where there is a small lake called Loughnashade, 'the lake of the treasures', which may recall ancient unrecorded finds. The landscape to the east of Navan Fort has been removed by a large limestone quarry now, thankfully, halted but as yet unreclaimed.

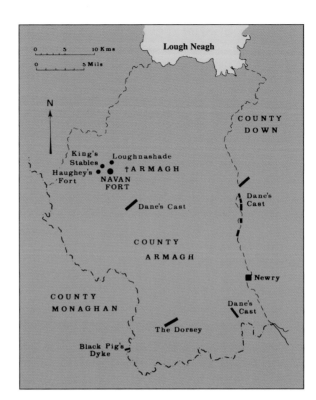

Fig. 3—Location map of Navan Fort.

Fig. 4—Aerial view of Navan Fort from the north-west. The Site B mound is on the hilltop inside the large enclosure. Site A is above, closer to the centre of the enclosure.

At one point on the north, the ditch and bank run across the top of the hill, but on the south beside the road they descend almost to the base of the hill. The earthwork is best preserved on the south-west (where it forms the route to the hilltop) but has been thoroughly levelled on the east, where the ditch exists as a broad hollow and the line of the inner face of the bank is marked by a hedge (also the boundary of the accessible part of the site). To the casual visitor the monument may not at first sight seem particularly impressive. Indeed, I have conducted groups to the top of the hill who then asked 'where is the fort?'. But the view from the top is unexpectedly wide, especially to the north, where across Lough Neagh Slemish Mountain, Co. Antrim, can be seen on a fine day. To the east the cathedrals of the old City of Armagh are prominent. To the south-east and south the skyline is formed by the low mountains of south Armagh (Sliab Fuaid), with the site of a large prehistoric passage tomb known as the 'Vicar's Cairn' at the northern end.

The modern approach to the hilltop follows the curving line of the earthwork ditch on the west, but this was not an ancient entrance. The bottom of the ditch was probably about 3m or 4m below the present surface of the hollow marking its line, but silting, erosion and peat growth over the centuries have gradually filled it up. The once-continuous bank runs parallel to the ditch downslope to the west. Where best preserved, the bank is some 15m wide and 4m high. As with other earthworks, we should try to imagine the larger mass and steeper profile of the monument when it was first built, before erosion and cultivation gradually ground it down. Why did people come to this pleasant place at some time in prehistory and build a huge circular enclosure almost a kilometre in external circumference? Why did their grassy monument remain famous as Emain Macha, a place to be celebrated in an early literary tradition as an ancient capital?

There are two other monuments visible on the hilltop encircled by the earthworks delimiting the sanctuary or 'fort'. The first, designated 'Site A' in the 1960s excavations, is a ploughed-down, late prehistoric ceremonial or burial monument, known as a 'ring-barrow', relatively uncommon in Ireland. The second, 'Site B', is a large artificial mound 6m high, and it too was largely excavated in the 1960s. Before excavation the mound could not easily be classified as belonging to a particular type of monument, nor could it readily be assigned to a particular period in the past. Perhaps it was thought to be a passage tomb, a type of Neolithic burial mound already known from the 1950s excavations to exist in Tara, Co. Meath, a site in many ways comparable to Navan. This mound is the most prominent feature of the site, and its unusual construction as revealed by Waterman's excavations from 1963 to 1971 is the main stimulus for writing this book. The mound dominates the whole hilltop, but it was impossible to say whether the visible monuments were of the same age or to be sure that other significant features had not been levelled beyond recognition in the past. The position of the original entrance or entrances to Navan Fort remains a matter for speculation. Stretches of the earthworks have been levelled, and any of the gaps in better-preserved sections may be of relatively modern origin, created for farm access or by removal of soil. Waterman suspected that the original entrance, if indeed there was one, might lie at the bottom of the hill, somewhere in the eastern sector.

The site and mound were first described by John O'Donovan, who collected information on historical sites and place-names for the Ordnance Survey in 1835:

> Nothing now appears but two outer ramparts and a fosse or ditch comprising an area of about eleven Irish acres, inside which are to be seen a moat [Site B, mound] commanding a most extensive prospect of the country in every direction, and a rath [Site A] of no remarkable size: the temptation which the ramparts of Emania hold out to the manuring eye of the farmer, will soon level it with the field, and render it a smoothly cultivated hill.

A plan of Navan Fort made at the same time by H. Tucker of the Royal Engineers shows, however, that the monument survives to this day much as it did then (Fig. 5). O'Donovan noted that 'There is a large piece of the mound of the inner fort dug and mixt with lime to be spread out on the field for the next crop...I observed the lime on the stones dug up.' Before the mound was excavated there was a pronounced hollow on its northern side, which may have been created by the operation he described. The interest shown in the monument by the first Ordnance Survey may have contributed to stopping the ongoing levelling. Otherwise the mound would have been taken away and the key piece of information for the interpretation of the site would have gone. The significance of his reference to 'stones dug up' will become clear later.

Within Ireland the best comparisons for the Navan monuments in terms of scale

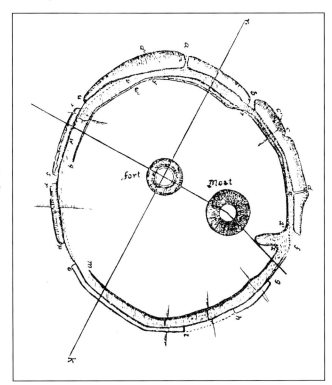

Fig. 5—Ordnance Survey plan of Navan Fort, c. 1835; north is to the bottom. 'Fort' is Site A and 'Moat' is Site B.

and layout are provided by two of the other sites with provincial 'royal' associations, Tara, Co. Meath, and Knockaulin, Co. Kildare. Tara is on the top of a long, gently sloping ridge with extensive views to the west across the rolling midlands. The summit is encircled by the remains of a large oval earthwork with a bank downslope from the ditch. The enclosure is called the 'Fort of the Kings' (Ráith na Ríg) and measures some 380m north–south by 300m east–west. There are three other upstanding monuments within the enclosure, two of which may be large barrows (later prehistoric burial monuments). The third is a prominent but not large passage tomb called the 'Mound of the Hostages' (Dumha na nGiall). It is said to have been associated with the large pillar-stone called the 'Stone of Destiny' (Lia Fáil) now in one of the possible barrows (Fig. 6).

The prominent hill of Knockaulin near Kilcullen, Co. Kildare, was identified by John O'Donovan in 1837 as Dún Ailinne, a place referred to in documents of the medieval period and traditionally regarded as the seat of the kingship of the province of Leinster and as a symbol of that kingship. The hill is encircled by a massive earthwork, subcircular on plan. It measures 460m north–south and 370m east–west and consists of a massive bank, downslope of the ditch from which it was quarried, with an entrance on the eastern side. The top of the hill was occupied in O'Donovan's time by a 'little internal rath', suggesting the presence of a smaller monument, possibly a barrow like those at Navan Fort and Tara. Thus three of the main sites traditionally associated with the early kingship of Irish provinces share a number of monumental features, primarily a large earthwork enclosure of roughly circular outline with the bank external to, or downslope from, the ditch. Although there are other earthwork enclosures of this scale known in Ireland, they have significant differences from the monuments at the so-called royal sites. For example, the Giant's Ring at Ballynahatty on the outskirts of Belfast is another earthwork monument of similar scale to Navan Fort (and is more completely preserved), but it lacks legendary or historical notice, occupies a level site, apparently has no ditch and has the remains of a megalithic tomb near the centre.

Archaeologists classify monuments and artefacts, initially on the basis of their appearance, into groups that have features in common. Not only does this aid description and discussion but there is also an implicit assumption that sites (and objects) of the same type were used for similar purposes and at around the same time in the past. The time-span of main use may not have been long. This enables data obtained by excavation at one site of the class, perhaps demonstrating its age or function, to be extended with caution to other, unexplored sites of the same 'type'. Sometimes, however, further research shows that sites that appear to be superficially similar should not have been considered as members of a unified group. But the earthworks at Tara, Navan and Knockaulin, coupled with the historical traditions associated with them, suggest that these three sites were enclosed at around the same time. What that time was is another question. Since the monuments were classed as 'hillforts', and hillforts in the 1960s were believed to date from the Early Iron Age, the major period of construction and use of the sites was believed to have been somewhere between 400 BC and AD 200.

This broad date suited a section of scholarly opinion that saw elements of the

Fig. 6—Aerial view of the Tara monument complex from the south (photo: The Discovery Programme).

early medieval (that is, seventh- to twelfth-century) traditions about these monumental sites as a genuine inheritance from the pagan past. An older generation of antiquaries may even have considered that there was an element of real history in the myths and sagas associated with the monuments and that the named kings and heroes of old did indeed live in palaces at these sites. Nowadays, one attempts to start from the assumption that there is unlikely to be any direct connection between mythic or legendary lore and the archaeological remains that may exist at the sites in question. Indeed, it is only with great caution that it is possible to equate recorded events, such as sackings or burnings, with archaeological layers found in historical settlements such as towns or castles, where the identification of historical events should be easier.

Normally in a short publication about a major historical monument the legendary, mythological and historical information about the site would be summarised at this stage. But, as well as explaining something about the discoveries made in and around Navan Fort, I hope to outline how ideas about the site have evolved and are still evolving. An introduction to the mythological and literary traditions centring on Navan will, therefore, be deferred until later. As we will see, the circumstances that gave rise to the 1960s excavations meant that the team involved did not approach the site of Navan Fort primarily from the point of view of research into a late prehistoric provincial sanctuary. The possibility that there were archaeological insights to be found in the literature and legend associated with the site was not the starting point for research. Although 'Celtic' scholars like Deirdre Flanagan of Queen's University were kept well informed about discoveries at Navan, it is true to say that, given the straightforward remit of the project (to excavate the mound), literary research made little contribution to the ongoing interpretation of the remains being uncovered. Perhaps this was a good thing, because the excavation was conducted in a completely objective manner and the archaeological remains were interpreted on their own merits as tangible features. Any subsequent interpretations of the remains uncovered based on literary traditions about the site cannot have been prejudiced by the archaeologists mistakenly 'discovering' what they had hoped or expected to find. Preconceived ideas can influence excavation strategy and on-site interpretation. Still, when conducting excavations at such a significant site, it is important to open the mind to the widest possible range of interpretations in case aspects of them can be tested while the archaeological deposits that enable this to be done survive.

The Archaeological Survey of Northern Ireland was set up in 1950, and the job of the two archaeologists it employed, Waterman and Collins, was to survey all the known monuments and archaeological sites of Northern Ireland, creating records of them and publishing most of the information with drawings and photographs of selected monuments in volumes on a county basis. The initial survey of County Armagh was completed before the end of the 1950s, and several excavations arising from the fieldwork had been carried out on prehistoric monuments, notably Annaghmare court tomb, Ballykeel portal tomb and Slieve Gullion passage tomb. With a view to completing a modest research programme, in the early 1960s D.M. Waterman prepared a shortlist of unusual monuments in the county that he thought would repay small-scale excavation. Navan Site A was on the list. It was described as a small circular earthwork with external bank. Maybe it was thought to be a variant form of Early Christian period rath or enclosed farmstead, the commonest type of field antiquity in Ireland. The real question was 'why should there be an ordinary rath inside a larger monument evidently of much greater prestige?'.

Site A

Archaeological excavation involves the removal of layers and features from the top down, in the reverse order of their deposition. This is a logical procedure, and it allows the full extent of every deposit to be recorded before it is removed. The success of the process naturally depends on the team's ability to recognise and record the subtle differences between one archaeological layer and another. Excavation trenches are marked out in areas where answers to the questions posed by the 'research design' for the excavation may be expected. The soil in them is then stripped off in thin layers, and the pattern (extent, depth and nature) of successive underlying deposits is recorded on scaled plans, notebooks and photographs. Samples may be removed for laboratory studies, and each deposit recognised is given a unique number to enable correlation of the archive and finds during and after the excavation.

The excavation of Site A took place in the summer of 1961 as a relatively routine component of the ongoing survey of the monuments of County Armagh. The centre of the ringwork lies approximately 30m south-east of the centre of the Navan enclosure, at the south-east edge of the flat summit. The main feature now visible is a wide hollow forming a large ring on plan. This marks the line of a largely filled-in ditch some 30m in diameter and 2m deep. The appearance of the centre of the monument as a low mound was probably produced by ploughing down the edges of the central area into the ditch. There are slight traces of an external bank on the north and west. When originally complete, the bank would have been about 50m in diameter crest to crest. The monument was sometimes described as a rath (a habitation site of the Early Christian period, dating from AD 600–900), but the small internal area, external bank and lack of an entrance causeway make it more likely that this was a later prehistoric ceremonial monument.

The excavation did not reveal much new information about the visible monument of Site A itself. The discovery of part of a bronze brooch (Fig. 7) of the Early Christian period in the ditch fill perhaps heightened the impression that the monument was a rath, but recent radiocarbon dating of animal bones found at a lower level in the fill shows that the monument was much older than this date. Of great interest, however, was the discovery of a large circular feature that pre-dated the earthwork of Site A.

Underneath the remnant of the bank of Site A and cut through by its ditch, Waterman and his team found an unusual series of three concentric circular trenches, which he defined as 'Phase A '(Fig. 8). These were easy to recognise as soon as the topsoil was removed because the soil they were filled with contrasted with the brown subsoil they were cut into. The soil layers filling the features were varied and complex. The trenches were flat bottomed and steep sided in profile. The

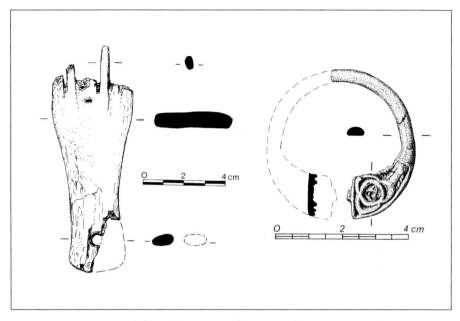

Fig. 7—Weaving-comb from the interior of Site A and bronze brooch from the ditch of Site A.

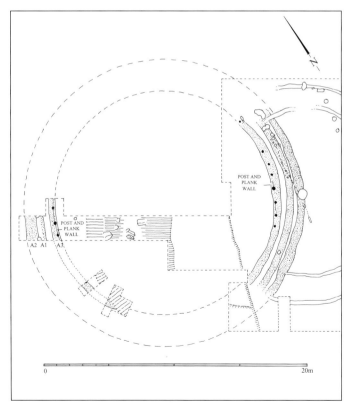

Fig. 8—A plan of the circular structure, defined by three wall-trenches, found under Site A in 1961.

outer one was almost 20m in diameter and 0.75m deep. The excavation showed that the trenches were originally dug, and perhaps abandoned, in sequence, the middle one first, then the outer and finally the inner. The outer edge of the middle trench had been cut away by the inner edge of the outer trench, establishing the sequence between these two.

The soil filling the trenches suggested that the innermost was a foundation slot for a wall of heavy timbers, but the contents of the middle and outer trenches were different. The outer one contained a striking deposit of highly burnt soil running down its inner edge, and the fill of the middle trench was relatively undistinguished, with no sign of sockets for timbers or walling. The innermost trench, however, contained vertical columns of soft dark soil, representing the positions of rotted-out timbers, that contrasted with the redeposited subsoil packed into the trench around them. These features were spaced about 1m apart and are known as 'post-pipes', where vertical timber posts had rotted away and were gradually replaced by dark soil mainly deposited by worms and rootlets. These were linked by a narrow vertical seam of dark soil, which did not penetrate as deeply into the lower fill of the trench. This may represent the lowest course of wall-cladding, perhaps of split wooden planking. No sign of an entrance or door to the structure was uncovered, but this probably lay to the east, in the area cut away by the ditch of the earthwork, Site A.

The walls of many ancient wooden buildings were made this way. Their upright elements were embedded in the earth, either in continuous slots or trenches, as here in Site A, or in spaced post-holes, dug out singly for the purpose of securing upright timbers. Some of the subsoil would have been repacked into the hole around the post. These trenches under Site A were of very large scale but presumably marked the site of three large, circular, roofed buildings, constructed and removed in the sequence of the slots. Even more surprising was the discovery of a few fragments of Bronze Age coarse pottery around the slots and indeed in their fills, giving a clear indication of their date. At the base of the topsoil within Site A, an even rarer object was recovered. This was a piece of antler with teeth created by sawing parallel slots into one end. It is a type of object called a 'weaving-comb', although some have questioned whether this was their real purpose (Fig. 7). The interest of the comb, however, is that the type is characteristic of the Early Iron Age. While these artefacts are relatively common in parts of Britain, this is only the second one to have been found in Ireland. Although it was from the area of Site A, it was found at the base of the topsoil and so could not be positively linked to the construction or use of the Site A monument or of the features found in it. It provided, however, the first excavated evidence of activity on the hilltop during the mysterious and elusive Iron Age (see time-line, Fig 23).

The excavation of Site A, therefore, revealed clear evidence for the existence at Navan of unexpectedly large wooden buildings, probably of Late Bronze Age date. It suggested that human settlement, or at least activity, of high status took place at this time but of course did nothing to pin down the date of Navan Fort itself. The monument, Site A, was probably a ring-barrow and was clearly later in date than the Bronze Age features it cut away or covered. As far as Waterman was concerned at the end of 1961, that was the end of excavations in Navan Fort, and the following winter he drafted a report on Site A that unfortunately was never published. The drawings he prepared have survived and were published in the main report on Site B in 1997, but his typescript on Site A, which I had seen and discussed with him, did not turn up among his many papers after his death in 1979. The significance of the concentric trenches found under Site A is such that we had new reasons to re-excavate parts of them some 40 years after the completion of the 1961 excavation (see p. 98).

Chapter 2

Excavation of the mound:
into the unknown

The mound called Site B dominates the summit of the hill in Navan Fort and is visible from many points in the surrounding landscape. It lies about halfway between the centre of the enclosure and its perimeter, the line of the ditch on the west (Fig. 9). Before excavation the mound was 6m high and 50m in diameter. It was evenly rounded with a slightly flat top. Some thought that the hollow on the north resulted from an antiquarian excavation, but I tend to think of O'Donovan's 'large piece of the inner mound…dug…'. There is a relatively recent hedge bank around the base of the mound.

Why did the excavation on Site B begin, given that the completion of the work on Site A marked the end of the Archaeological Survey's exploration in Navan Fort? The Navan lore maintains that at a gathering in Oxford a representative of a US excavation team, funded by a Mr John Dimick and based in the University Museum, Pennsylvania, met Professor E.M. (Martyn) Jope of the Department of Archaeology, Queen's University, Belfast. When Jope heard that the Museum was looking for a Bronze Age site to excavate in Europe, he suggested that they should come to Navan Fort. No doubt it was the recent discovery of Bronze Age material under Site A that prompted this suggestion. Subsequent events leading up to the excavation were recorded by Waterman in his report:

> Mr Dimick agreed that a joint excavation by the University Museum, the Department of Archaeology in the Queen's University, Belfast, and the Archaeological Survey should be undertaken in the following year. The work was to be financed largely by the University Museum, with smaller contributions from Queen's University and the Ministry. A large mound, the second of the two features within Navan Fort, which had been interpreted as a passage grave or later burial monument, was proposed as a possible site for excavation. This

Fig. 9—The mound (Site B) in Navan Fort (photo: J. Finegan).

choice was approved by the Board of the University Museum, and their decision was conveyed to the Ministry by Mr Dimick. Accordingly excavation of the mound was commenced in June–July 1963 by students from the University of Pennsylvania under the leadership of Professor Bernard Wailes, and from the Queen's University of Belfast under Mr B C S Wilson and Mr S G Rees-Jones, supported by a small team of labourers previously employed on the excavation of site A. Overall responsibility was entrusted to the writer [Waterman], assisted by Mr A E P Collins.

Site B

In the first summer of excavation in 1963 a row of eleven 3.35m by 3.35m trenches was excavated across the mound (Fig. 10). At the lower ends the trenches were extended outward to investigate a sunken feature running around the base of the mound. This first season of excavation showed that the upper part of the mound was a thick layer of disturbed topsoil, not surprising as aerial photographs taken before excavation show broad cultivation ridges running over it. Beneath the topsoil was a deep deposit of horizontally layered soils and turves, deliberately dumped. From the different composition of the many thin and extensive layers, it was clear that not all of them could have come from the top of the Navan drumlin. For example, some of the lower layers were compressed peat, which must have come from a damp environment elsewhere.

The mound

Altogether, the topsoil and underlying mixed deposits were some 2.5m deep at the

Fig. 10—The first trench cut into the mound summit in 1963 (photo J. Delmege).

centre of the mound. They extended east and west across the mound, but the trial excavation of 1963 also showed that the outer profile of the mound had been formed by dumping a continuous stack of turves or sods around its perimeter. This turf stack was built just before the dumping of the soil and layers of turves that formed the central body of the mound. The perimeter turf bank, therefore, both formed and contained the mound. We have no way of knowing how steep the original mound edge was because many centuries of weathering and cultivation have probably reduced its profile considerably. There were no finds in the soil layers forming the upper slopes of the mound.

We noted earlier that the mound was over 5m high, but the soil layers were only some 2.5m thick. What gave the mound bulk under the soil? The first season of excavation demonstrated that right across the mound, along the broad east–west section examined, the soil layers rested on top of a layer of boulders. Indeed, because the layer of stones sloped down to the ground level of the hilltop under the outer mantle of soil at both sides, it was concluded that the stones represented the top of a substantial cairn or mound of limestone boulders. This was an unusual discovery, but the excavators may yet have retained in mind the possibility that they were dealing with a passage tomb because the Mound of the Hostages in Tara, shown to be a Neolithic passage tomb in the 1950s excavations, had a similar construction, an inner core of boulders capped by a thick layer of clay. But before the 1963 excavation finished an even more surprising feature was uncovered.

At the mound edges (at the opposite ends of the excavated trial section) a slot or narrow trench was found on the level of the surrounding hilltop. This was filled with contrasting darker soil and was cut into the layers on which the boulders rested. The slot hugged the outer edge of the stone cairn and apparently enclosed it in a circle 40m in diameter. The feature was found at opposite ends of the excavated diameter and was presumed to have continued all around the cairn. In the western end of the section a large post-pit was found that lay in the line of the encircling slot. Fragments of an upright oak post survived in the pit. It appeared that the relatively shallow slot marked the site of some form of wooden walling, held up by large posts inserted into spaced post-pits. The wooden wall appeared to have delimited, indeed even contained, the outer face of the cairn of loose boulders (Fig. 11). Outside the wall, and apparently pre-dating the mound, a wide shallow ditch filled with silt and occupation soil was uncovered. No evidence was found in this first season that would help to date the sequence of unusual structures uncovered.

In summary, the evidence recorded in 1963 showed a sequence of undated, but presumably prehistoric, events on the hilltop. First the people dug a ditch some 5m wide, 1m deep and about 45m in diameter, which afterwards silted up gradually over a lengthy period. Then, roughly concentric with the early ditch, they or their

Fig. 11—Navan mound in 1963, showing the outer edge of the buried cairn and a post-pit of the surrounding wooden wall.

successors erected a wooden wall, probably supported on spaced timber uprights. After building the wooden wall, they heaped up a cairn of stones, filling the space surrounded by the wall, which remained standing. Otherwise the correspondence between the line of the wall and the lower edge of the cairn would not have been so close. There were some indications that the wooden wall had burned (deposits of charcoal and burnt earth), but the final act in the sequence of mound-building was the covering in of the cairn of stones with deep layers of earth, clay, turves and redeposited subsoil. Thus the first season of excavation had demonstrated the main stages in construction of the large mound that had survived, in eroded form, until 1963. But even more intriguing details and constructions were to emerge in further seasons of digging.

For reasons that are not entirely clear, in subsequent years of summer excavation the dig was carried out solely by the Ministry of Finance under the direction of D.M. Waterman, assisted by Stephen Rees-Jones of Queen's University and with the support of the Historic Monuments Advisory Council. It appears that Waterman was informed with regret in the winter of 1963–4 that the funding for the Pennsylvania team had dried up and that they could no longer participate. In 1964 and 1965 the earth mound covering the cairn was removed (Fig. 12). The outer part of the mound was excavated as a series of radial cuttings to permit study of the sod stack running around the slope of the mound. These two seasons of work confirmed the conclusions about the nature of the earth mound, its varied layers and the continuous nature of the containing stack of sods around the perimeter. No finds were made in the soil layers, and there were no internal structures in the mound.

There were two major discoveries at this time. It became clear that the wooden

Fig. 12—Removing the earth mound from the surface of the cairn, 1964.

wall around the outer, basal edge of the cairn had burned down after the cairn was built but before the earth mound was heaped over it. Everywhere around the perimeter there were traces of burning overlying the site of its foundation trench, and there were remains of charred timbers at places on the lower slopes of the cairn. Indeed, at one point the edge of the cairn had evidently been built up against the wall because it had spilled outward when the wall burned. This collapse preserved traces of a burnt wall-beam underneath as a band of charcoal, which was identified as an oak plank (or the charred surface of an oak beam). The plank must have been the lowest part of the wall lying in the shallow foundation gully at the edge of the cairn.

The fact that the wall had burned all around the edge of the cairn suggested that the fire was deliberate. How could an accidental fire have started and how could it have burned so consistently all around the 40m-diameter cairn? At one point, where the cairn had collapsed outward on burning, the stones appeared to have prematurely extinguished bundles of twigs placed against the wall of the building. They were preserved as groups of parallel strands of charcoal. This was interpreted by Waterman as evidence that kindling had been deliberately placed against the outside of what he concluded was a wall of oak planks or beams to make sure that it burned thoroughly and completely.

The other major discovery was that when the top of the cairn was fully exposed it was found to be almost flat, rather than domed, and that the surface was divided into a series of wedges of various sizes radiating from the centre. The wedges were distinguished from one another by a variety of features: differences in the sizes of the boulders used in adjacent segments; aligned kerbs of larger boulders radiating from the centre and forming the edges of wedges; slight differences in height between adjacent wedges; and sometimes linear hollows between them. The width and distribution of the wedges were not uniform, the existence and location of some being apparent only on the aerial photograph taken of the excavated cairn surface (Fig. 13). The reason for the formation of these radial divisions was not apparent. Clearly, the outline of the cairn was determined by the wooden wall containing it, and its designers must have decided on the flat-topped profile. If the cairn was built in one huge operation, we would not expect this radial arrangement to have been created accidentally. It looked like a deliberate surface treatment. During the excavation it was suggested that the cairn was built by different groups of workers bringing stones from a variety of locations and that the wedges were created more or less accidentally in apportioning different areas for them to build so as not to get in one another's way.

A long time was spent by Waterman at the end of the 1965 season preparing a meticulous, stone-by-stone survey and plan of the exposed cairn surface. In 1966 the southern two-thirds of the cairn was removed and dumped in an arc to the south and west of the mound. The excavated spoil from the sod mound had been dumped on the hilltop on the north. By the end of the 1966 season the mound had virtually disappeared, and its site was overlooked by the curving embankment of excavated spoil. On the northern side, about 1m in height of the cairn was left unexcavated in order to preserve undisturbed information for future research.

Fig. 13—Surface of the cairn from the air showing radial divisions (photo: N. Mitchel).

The cairn and the wooden building

Presumably it was thought that the excavation of the limestone cairn would be a relatively routine, if somewhat laborious, operation. The workers found that the stones were of a variety of sizes, from cobble up to about football size being the average, but there were larger ones. Most of the stones could be carried to a wheelbarrow, sometimes with difficulty, by two men. Most of the stones were fossiliferous limestone boulders from the immediate locality, but there were a few erratic boulders of different stone. Samples of these were collected for study at the time of excavation, but their location is now unknown. From conversation, I know that Waterman was puzzled by the nature of the boulders. Where had they come from? Having been protected from percolating water by the covering mound, they were as well preserved as the day they were dumped by the original builders. But the stones were somewhat rounded, not sharp and angular as they would have been if freshly quarried. During the excavation there was a general assumption that the ditch forming the main enclosure was dug at the same time as the mound was built. In some places the edges of the ditch are rock cut, and a considerable volume of limestone could have become available as a result of cutting the ditch through these areas. Because limestone becomes deeply fissured when exposed to the elements, Waterman thought that most of the stones may have been snapped off a weathered outcrop in the vicinity or that they were glacially rounded boulders that are found in the sand and clay capping of the local drumlins. Many such boulders would have been found in digging the main enclosure.

But the strangest thing discovered during the removal of the cairn had been built before a single boulder was dumped on the site. Not long after the team of excavators had begun to strip off the upper surface of the cairn, suddenly the top of a small vertical void appeared. A few stones were lifted away from one spot, and a dark cavity appeared, about 40cm in diameter, running down into the body of the cairn. Its base was below arm's length, and probing with a pole showed that the vertical void extended down into the body of the cairn to its full depth. The end of the probe went into sticky mud below the base of the cairn. The team had no ready explanation for this feature, which would have been very difficult for the cairn builders to construct deliberately. It could not have formed after the cairn was built because it was protected from disturbance by the sod mound. The weight and gritty surfaces of the limestone blocks would have prevented them from moving around after they had been dumped by the mound-builders.

The extraordinary explanation for the feature suddenly became clear when, as the work of stripping the cairn continued, other voids or vertical cavities were uncovered. They were located at various depths in the cairn body but always ran down as rough vertical cylinders to a sticky clay underneath the base of the cairn (demonstrated by probing and measuring). The voids were evidently caused by the rotting of large, vertical timber posts around which the cairn had been packed when it was built. When the posts rotted away, the gritty surfaces of the stones, despite various pressures in the cairn body, prevented them from slipping into the developing cavities. As a result, vertical open 'pipes' remained, showing where the individual posts once stood. It appeared that some movement was possible in the upper part of the cairn below the earth mound and that the cavities had sometimes been closed by slipping stones pressed in by the weight of the clay and other soils above. In general it appeared that the timbers originally extended higher than the level at which they were first recognised in the cairn.

As the removal of the cairn continued downwards and the positions of the post-voids were plotted on plan, it became clear that the upright posts were arranged in four circles concentric with the wooden wall encircling the base of the cairn. A realisation dawned that the cairn had been placed inside a *huge standing wooden building* formed of rings of very substantial posts and was not simply encased in the outer wall first identified in 1963. Nothing like this had ever been recognised in an excavation before. If this was a building, it would be the largest single integrated wooden structure known in prehistoric Ireland. There was no recognised monument type to which the Navan mound could be assigned, and there was still no evidence of the date and purpose of the extraordinary structure. But the strange sequence of mound construction was by now clear:

1. First, after clearing away remains of earlier structures, the builders erected a huge timber building 40m in diameter. It had four main rings of posts and a solid outer wall. There was as yet no direct evidence of how, or even if, it was roofed.
2. Then they packed limestone boulders inside the structure to a height of nearly 3m, forming a flat-topped cairn.
3. Then they deliberately burned the wooden structure containing and covering the

cairn. They probably tidied away the exposed remains of the building, apart from charred pieces of the wall trapped and covered where the cairn had collapsed over at the edges. Although the post-voids did not often reach the top of the cairn, we suspect that originally the posts may have protruded above it.

4. Finally, the mound-builders covered the cairn and the remains of the timber building with the capping layers of turves and varied subsoils, some of which seem to have been brought to the site from elsewhere.

5. Presumably the builders and their descendants continued to use the monument complex they had created for some generations, but these subsequent activities have left few traces.

Chapter 3

Iron Age wooden buildings:
palaces or temples?

Underneath the cairn

The removal of the central and southern area of the cairn enabled excavation of the pre-cairn levels. The work was carried out over four summer seasons from 1967 to 1970. In each season a separate area, or 'quadrant', was completely excavated. It was hoped that finds and other material on the 'floor' of the wooden building (the surface or ground on which it was built) would make clear what its date and purpose were. Was there a richly furnished burial at its centre? Was it a temple? But in fact the excavations under the mound deepened the puzzles of the Navan story, added further evidence to the intriguing history of the mound, and extended the complicated story of human activity on the site backwards in time from the construction of the mound. The excavation of the post-pits (more than 200 of them) of the wooden building in the subsoil under the mound had to be completed, and its internal ground surface or floor had to be examined carefully.

When the stones forming the bottom of the cairn were removed, they were found to be lying on a layer of clean, sticky, yellowish-red clay (some 5–10cm thick), which covered about three-quarters of the area under the cairn and formed the 'floor' of the timber building. Indeed, it was thought for a while to have been deliberately laid as the floor of the structure. No artefacts or traces of other activity were found in or on the yellow clay. In the areas where the clay layer did not exist, it was clear that the cairn stones rested on the surface of a (deep) layer of dark soil containing much of what appeared to be occupation rubbish (bone scraps and charcoal) that ran under the clay and, therefore, pre-dated it and had nothing to do with either the timber structure or the composite mound.

Further excavation showed that the yellow clay had not been deliberately laid as a floor. The numerous post-pits of the wooden building were so large and deep that they penetrated deep into the clean subsoil. This upcast subsoil had been piled on the ground surface beside each post-hole after it had been carefully dug out. When the wooden post was put in the hole by the builders of the structure, it took up so much room that it was possible only to re-pack less than half of the upcast from the hole back into it. The result was that there were small heaps of unused clean clay to get rid of, and the builders simply spread it out roughly on the ground between the posts. So no evidence was found for any activity in the timber building: it was put up; the yellow clay was spread out; and, apparently immediately, the cairn was put inside it.

The multi-ring timber building, or '40-metre structure'

The wooden building was in many ways the most spectacular discovery of this phase of the Navan excavation (Fig. 14). The full excavation of its southern two-thirds in the pre-cairn ground surface revealed many interesting details about its construction. The huge structure was about 40m in diameter. Its main wall of horizontal timbers was held up by 34 pairs of posts set in large pits 3.5m apart. In

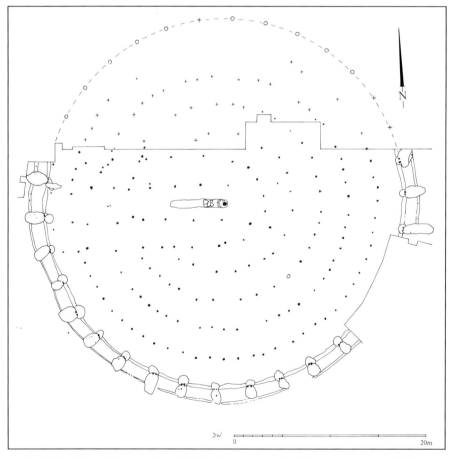

Fig. 14—Plan of the wooden building known as the '40-metre structure'. Each black dot represents a vertical post.

turn this wall was encircled by a narrower trench or slot 1m further out that seems to have held a fence to define the building site during construction but did not hold any of the completed structure. Inside the building were four concentric rings, 3m apart, of upright posts. The post-holes had all contained columns of dark soil in the centre of their packing, showing where the large post in each pit had rotted away. The diameter of the posts was confirmed at about 30cm by the discovery of post-butts (all of oak) in the bases of some of the post-sockets, which were generally between 70cm and 90cm deep. This was because the cairn and mound caused the natural water table (the level below which the ground remains generally wet) in the subsoil to rise under it, preserving some of the deeper timbers. The rounded post-butts had been cut with a metal-bladed axe, showing that the structure could not date from before the Bronze Age, a significant insight in itself.

On the western side of the building the circular arrangement of posts gave way to four parallel rows running in from the outer wall to the centre of the structure, forming what Waterman termed an 'ambulatory', a feature used for processions at the eastern end of some large medieval churches. The ambulatory consisted of three parallel 'aisles' focusing on a huge isolated post at the centre of the building. The central post was 50cm in diameter, and its butt survived down in the damp subsoil to a length of 1.4m. It was in fact the trunk of a sizeable oak tree, retaining multiple axe-marks from its felling (Fig. 15). The post was evidently so long and heavy that, in order to raise it, the builders made a ramp 6m long, sloping into the bottom of

Fig. 15—Axe-trimmed butt of the central post from the wooden building.

the pit from the west. The post, therefore, must have been at least 12m long and would have stood more than 10m high at the top of the hill. This huge post was unnecessary for the structural stability of the timber building (whatever way it was built). It clearly had some ceremonial purpose, underlined by the way the ambulatory was aligned around it at the centre of the building. Perhaps it was venerated like a kind of totem pole.

The existence of the central post and its relation to the rest of the building raise questions that we skirted around earlier but that were in the forefront of Waterman's concerns during the excavation. Was there any evidence that the large timber structure carried a roof? Was the tall timber post inside a roofed building? Did the building have any roof at all? The burning around the edge of the cairn related only to the destruction of the outer wall of the building. The records in the excavation archive have no evidence for the remains of anything like a collapsed or burnt roof on top of the cairn, the logical position to find such remains. The most compelling evidence, however, for the existence of a roof or 'superstructure' came from some of the lowest points of the building: the bottoms of the post-holes dug to hold the upright posts tightly in place.

When the archaeologists excavated a post-hole of the timber structure, the procedure was first to remove the soft inner fill where the post had rotted away. The resulting void was measured from above in cross-section. Then the soil packing around the post was cross-sectioned and removed to expose the post-hole as originally excavated by the ancient builders. This painstaking process revealed that a number of posts in the building had been pushed down into the subsoil by as much as 10cm or 15cm below the bases of the sockets dug to receive them. This was strong evidence that the uprights were supporting considerably more than their own weight. The excavation team also discovered that all of the paired posts (34 pairs) around the perimeter of the timber building (in the line of its outer wall) had originally existed as only one post in each case. All of these single posts had similarly been pushed into subsoil below the bases of the sockets dug for them. The response of the builders to this evident sinkage in their new structure was to dig secondary pits sloping down from outside the building and to place a second upright beside every primary one, evidently to counteract the downward pressure. This expedient was not entirely successful, as many of the secondary posts were also pressed into the subsoil below the holes dug for them.

We do not hear of fence posts or even telegraph poles sinking into the ground of their own accord! In the unlikely event that a pile-driver was used to ram in the posts, the phenomenon would have been more widespread and the emergency addition of secondary posts around the outer wall would remain to be explained. It is clear that the sinking was caused by the weight the posts were carrying. This can only have been a roof, or at least a superstructure of some sort (Fig. 16). One might ask: why, if this was present, did all the posts not get pushed down? Probably the posts in the outer ring had to carry a greater load than the others because of their wider spacing. Perhaps the other posts in the inner rings and ambulatory that sunk did so because they were in isolated patches of marginally softer subsoil or because their ends were more pointed than their neighbours.

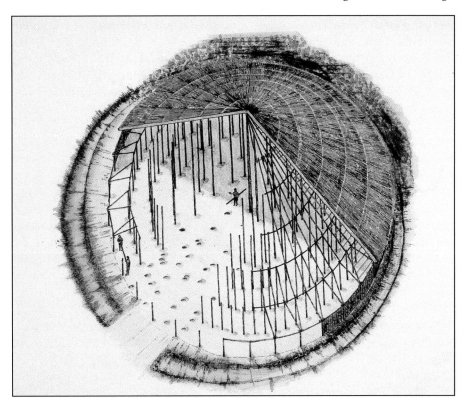

Fig. 16—A suggested reconstruction of the wooden building (D. Wilkinson).

Iron Age figure-of-eight structures under the mound

At this stage of the excavation the team was concentrating on the accurate recording of the large wooden structure rather than worrying too much about its interpretation. After all, they still did not know what age it was beyond the fact that it was prehistoric, in this case before about AD 400, and that it was later than the Early Bronze Age. But as the excavation of the post-sockets of the timber building proceeded in 1967 and 1968 it became clear that the timber building had been constructed on a surface that was the *top* of a series of accumulated deposits, representing a long phase of earlier occupation. When the excavation and recording of the post-pits of the timber building was complete, the underlying layers were excavated. They were 30–40cm thick and contained the remains of eleven foundation trenches for circular timber buildings. These were identical in layout to those found under Site A in 1963, thought at that time to date from the Bronze Age. These extraordinary buildings, from 10m to 13.5m in diameter, were smaller than the one at Site A. From the discovery that each had a central fireplace and associated domestic rubbish, they were assumed to be dwelling-houses. Like the structures under Site A, the foundation trenches under the mound occurred in groups of three concentric rings.

The excavation of these levels was very difficult because the architectural features cut into the dark occupation soil were often filled with identical material. Because so many buildings had been erected successively on the same site, their foundation slots frequently intersected (Fig. 17). Unfortunately, the fill of all the slots was very similar, making it difficult to work out which cut which. But, by careful study and recording of these intersections, Waterman was able to figure out the sequence of construction of all of the buildings. This was a very complicated task, and its successful accomplishment was a masterpiece of careful excavation technique and recording. The buildings under the mound had east-facing entrances and were attached to larger, circular slots on the north, thought to be outdoor enclosures or farmyards. The entire structure, therefore, had a figure-of-eight plan, but it was not always clear which 'house' was attached to which enclosure on the north. These 'yards' or roofless enclosures were entered from the houses on the south via simple gaps in the walling. The larger northern enclosures had wide 'main' entrances, possibly protected by gates, and were approached from the east by roughly parallel foundation slots. Traces of charred timberwork and post-voids in the slots show that some of them supported stout wooden fences or walls (Fig. 18).

Finds from the pre-mound levels
The construction method implied by using sets of three concentric wall-slots in sequence was not considered in detail until after completion of the fieldwork. More

Fig. 17—The south-west quadrant of the pre-mound surface during excavation showing Iron Age wall-slots cut by post-pits of the large wooden building (marked with white wands).

Fig. 18—An Iron Age palisade slot with the positions of posts marked with pegs.

important for the unfolding story of the excavation is the fact that dating evidence was beginning to come from the occupation layers on which the 40m structure was built. These dark layers of soil, compressed under the mound, contained specks of charcoal and red-burnt soil, along with hundreds of sherds of 'flat-rimmed ware', a type of coarse hand-made pottery. These crude, flat-bottomed vessels are believed to date from the middle or the end of the Bronze Age. Four small bronze objects, characteristic of the Late Bronze Age, were also revealed in the occupation soil: a socketed axehead, a tiny spearhead, a sickle blade and a mount from a scabbard (Fig. 19). These finds suggested that the pre-mound houses dated from the Late Bronze Age, perhaps around 600 BC. Since there was no evidence that much time had elapsed between the building of the last of the 'houses' and the construction of the 40m wooden building, it could have been concluded that the latter and the encasing mound also dated from the Bronze Age or a little later. The clay 'floor' of

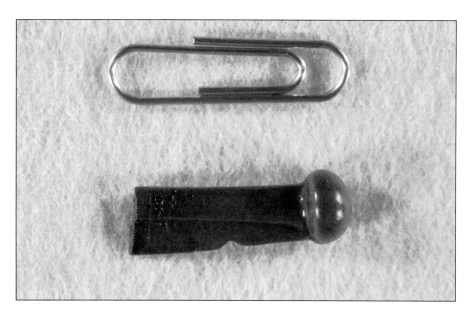

Fig. 19—Part of the decorated bronze terminal from the tip of a scabbard of 'Hallstatt' type, Late Bronze Age.

the 40m timber building dipped down into the fill of the latest of the gullies or wall-slots, showing that the wooden wall contained in the gully had decayed, or was perhaps even pulled out, not long before the clay was spread over during the construction of the large wooden building. A few other finds, however, showed that the settlement represented by the round houses carried on after the Bronze Age.

The occupation layers associated with the circular structures contained several iron objects. Some of these were nondescript scraps, but the purpose of two could be identified. One was a slender spoon-bit for drilling dowel- or peg-holes in wood, and the other (which, if memory serves correctly, I found while trowelling in 1969!) was a piece of binding, probably to hold the edges of two leather surfaces, for example at the edge of a scabbard or shield. These clearly showed that pre-mound occupation continued after the Bronze Age into the Early Iron Age, say, up to at least 300 BC. There was a suggestion, however, that the iron objects may have been imported from Britain, where they may have been made at an earlier date. One object, however, from the pre-mound layers was certainly made in Ireland during the Iron Age. This was a bronze pin with a ring-head decorated with cast, raised, spiralling bosses (Fig. 20). Six other pins of the same type have been found in Ireland, but this is the first to have been discovered in excavation. The 'plastic' artwork of cast ornament compares with that on other decorated Iron Age objects in Europe and has been termed 'La Tène' style, from the site in Switzerland where the material was first excavated in significant volume. The series of Irish pins to which this type belongs is not well dated, but discovery of this one in 1970 at least showed that the large timber building and mound were not constructed until after the beginning of the Early Iron Age, say, after 250 BC.

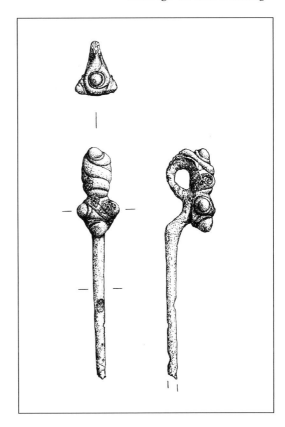

Fig. 20—Iron Age ring-headed pin decorated in La Tène style from the occupation layer under the mound (drawing: D. Warner; actual size).

The Bronze Age ring-ditch and post circle

The figure-of-eight structures were built under the mound during a period that seemed to span the transition from the Bronze Age to the Iron Age. This was regarded as very significant because it is a particularly obscure time in Irish prehistory, lacking archaeological evidence for sites and burials. There are relatively few objects from Ireland that can be dated securely to the period 500 BC to 250 BC, and no settlements of this period have been recognised and excavated. This is not to say that they did not exist, just that they have not been found yet. At Navan it appeared that Waterman had discovered a distinct form of house and settlement that spanned the period. Associated with the buildings was a mixture of object types that represented both periods. But, as these figure-of-eight structures were being excavated in the late 1960s, features and structures of an even earlier period were being revealed underneath the occupation soil, cut into the subsoil. One of these we encountered earlier: the 5m-wide ditch around the base of the mound found in the first season of excavation.

The ditch was found running in a wide circle outside the base of the mound everywhere within the area excavated. It clearly encircled the mound but was much older than it. The ditch was 45m in internal diameter, 5m wide and 1m deep. Excavation proved that it was older than the mound because the occupation soil buried under the mound—distinct layers of dark soil mixed with charcoal, scraps of animal bones and occasional sherds of coarse pottery—ran down into it on all sides and formed the bulk of its fill. The occupation layer developed during the time of the ring-slot house sequence (the figures of eight). Since there were at least eleven successive structures (three groups of three and one group of two) represented by the ring-slots, the ditch must have pre-dated the mound by at least 150 years. When the mound was built, apparently deliberately fitted within its circuit, the ditch can only have been a faint hollow. Nothing was found on the ditch bottom to give a clue to its purpose, and it had no internal bank. Ancient ditches, dug for whatever purpose, were usually accompanied by a bank that was often the primary feature desired by the builders. Because the excavation did not extend beyond the outer edge of the ditch, we do not know if it had an external bank. Its width and relative shallowness, as well as the possibility that there was an external bank, suggested that the ditch was not intended for defensive purposes. There was a pebble-paved causeway to provide access across the ditch on the eastern side. The palisade slots forming the entrances to the northern enclosures of the later phase of figure-of-eight structures flanked the earlier causeway as if their positioning was intended to recognise and commemorate its existence.

Yet further features probably belonged to this earliest structural period. Underneath the remains of the circular houses and their associated occupation soil was a series of deep pits packed with clay and stones that formed a ring concentric with the ditch but 3m inside its line. The pits were 4m apart on average and were wide in relation to their depth of 1–1.25m. Soft vertical hollows running deep into the pit fillings showed that in many cases they held sizeable vertical posts that had either rotted away or been pulled out (Fig. 21). This ring of post-pits, of which

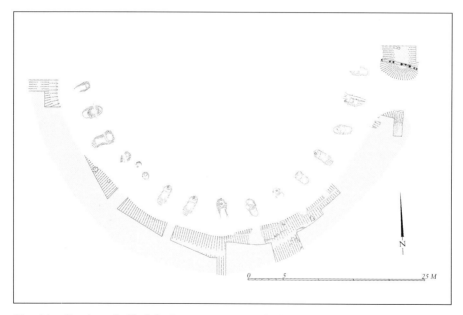

Fig. 21—Southern half of the Late Bronze Age ditched enclosure with the inner ring of post-pits.

fifteen were excavated, appears to have been associated with the early ditch, but there were no other traces of structures associated with them, for example in the form of a linking wall-trench or of further internal supports for a roofed building. It is possible that these posts simply stood in isolation and that, in conjunction with the ditch, they formed a ceremonial monument of unusual layout. When these features were first recognised, it was presumed, on grounds of symmetry and because the ring-slot houses appeared to be contained within the ring of posts, that the ditch was originally dug to delimit the site for the 'houses' and that the ring of timber posts held up a protective stockade that fell into decay at an early stage in the sequence of ring-slot houses. The features were, therefore, presumed to date from the Late Bronze Age, perhaps around 500 BC.

Only two earlier features or sets of features were uncovered. When all of the layers described above had been fully excavated a thin dark layer was exposed immediately overlying the surface of the subsoil right across the area excavated, except where it was cut away by archaeological features dug from above. This was interpreted as a ploughsoil or cultivation soil that existed before the cutting of the large ring-ditch. It was noticed that in certain areas the surface of the subsoil had been intersected by at least two sets of parallel shallow grooves crossing at right angles. The grooves were filled with dark sandy soil, interpreted as the base of a cultivated soil that existed on the hill before the construction of wooden buildings began in the Late Bronze Age. The criss-cross grooves were clearly produced by ancient ploughing, probably at some time in the Bronze Age (Fig. 22). The oldest feature recognised was a wide shallow pit that produced some sherds of Neolithic pottery, perhaps dating from around 3000 BC. A few other Neolithic finds, such as flint tools and broken pieces of ground stone axes, were found in layers of later date.

Summary and retrospect

We have reached the end of the main Site B excavation in 1970 and have surveyed everything that was exposed in the removal of the southern two-thirds of the mound. Now it is appropriate to summarise what was found in the reverse order of the excavation, that is, oldest first, most recent last (Fig. 23). The summary describes the evidence for the sequence of human activity on Site B running with time from the earliest to the latest. The information is listed with the phase numbers allocated to the structures and layers by Waterman as the excavation was nearing completion. Since the numbers logically should run from the earliest period to the latest, the beginning of the sequence has to be identified before phase numbers can be allocated. 'Phases' are separate groupings of remains or layers found on excavations that appear to represent coherent structures and characteristic patterns of activity in a recognisable sequential pattern. This should become clear below.

Phase 1: People were living or carrying out some activity on the hilltop in the Neolithic period. This was demonstrated by the discovery of flint scrapers, Neolithic pottery and fragments of stone axes in pre-mound deposits. One or two features cut into the subsoil apparently date from this period.

Fig. 22—Eastern side of the pre-mound subsoil surface showing criss-cross plough grooves (above the ranging rod).

Phase 2: Criss-cross grooves in the surface of the subsoil filled with sandy loam showed that the hilltop had been ploughed at some time in the Late Neolithic or the Bronze Age.

Phase 3 (i): The circular ditched enclosure was constructed, some 45m in diameter with an inner circle of 28 strong upright posts.

Phase 3 (ii): After the ditch had begun to silt up, the first of the series of figure-of-eight buildings or 'southern ring-slot enclosures' was built. This constructional phase must have lasted a considerable time, as there were ten rebuildings of the circular structure (Fig. 24). A thick occupation soil developed during this phase. It contained coarse pottery, animal bones, scraps of iron, and bronze and stone objects. Some were evidently churned up and redeposited from earlier phases.

Phase 3 (iii): This was distinguished by a marked shift to the north of the final three ring-slot enclosures. We know that this part of Phase 3, at least, extended into the Iron Age, after 250 BC.

Phase 4: This appears to have immediately followed Phase 3 (iii) and is the period of the construction and use of the 40m-diameter wooden structure. No artefacts or traces of any activities other than those connected with the construction were found in this phase.

Phase 5: This was the building of the cairn and the turfy mound. In a sense Phase 4 extended into Phase 5 because the wooden building was standing when the cairn was built. Phase 5 itself should be split in two by the burning (and demolition?) of those parts of the Phase 4 wooden building that were exposed

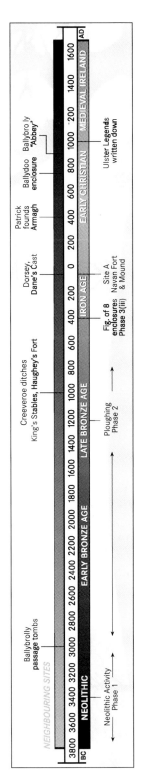

Fig. 23—Timeline showing main developments at Navan Fort and vicinity.

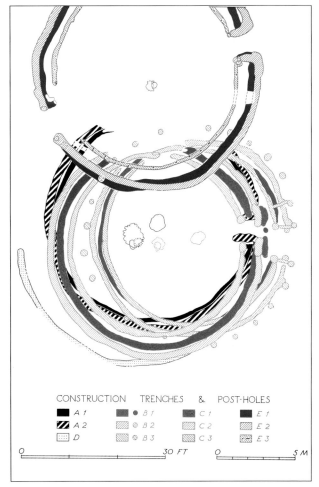

CONSTRUCTION TRENCHES & POST-HOLES

■ *A 1*	● *B 1*	*C 1*	■ *E 1*
▨ *A 2*	*B 2*	*C 2*	*E 2*
D	*B 3*	*C 3*	*E 3*

0   30 FT   0   5 M

Fig. 24—Plan of the pre-cairn surface showing the sequence of the sets of three concentric wall-slots.

above and around the cairn. This is the same point at which the builders changed from using stones to earth.

Phase 6: Although no evidence for it was found in excavation, we can presume that this phase existed as an important part of the human activity on the site: this was the intended and ongoing use of the mound by its builders after it was completed. This was the major question for consideration after the excavation. What was the mound built for?

Chapter 4

Post-excavation research: the mystery expands

Radiocarbon dating

It is well known that organic material, mainly wood, charcoal and bone, can be approximately dated by measuring the amount of a radioactive carbon isotope, carbon 14 (^{14}C for short), in the sample material. This procedure for age estimation depends on the fact that plants and animals during their lives absorb, from their food and respiration, known amounts of ^{14}C, which remains more or less at constant levels in the environment. The ^{14}C is produced by the interaction of solar radiation with ordinary carbon 12 in the upper atmosphere. When the plant or animal dies, it ceases to replace the radioactive ^{14}C, which has a half-life of about 5700 years (that is, after 5700 years half of the original quantity of ^{14}C remains). By measuring the amount of ^{14}C in the specimen it is possible to work out how much time has elapsed since the organism died. Archaeologists collect charcoal samples from layers and features that they would like to know the age of, and these are submitted to specialist laboratories to measure the minute proportion of ^{14}C in the carbon (Fig. 25). The laboratory produces a statistical statement for each sample to the effect that there is, for example, a 66% probability that the organism died between 100 bc and 200 bc, which would be stated as 150±50 bc. The 'dates' are 'calibrated' to adjust them for known fluctuations in the amount of ^{14}C in the environment at different times in the past, making them closer approximations to calendar years ('bc' is used for uncalibrated dates and 'BC' for calibrated (corrected) dates).

Uncertainties can arise, mainly concerned with the origins of the sample. Can we be sure that the organism being dated died shortly before it got into the feature being dated? Often the answer is 'No'. Imagine that a small tree has been felled (its ^{14}C content immediately starts to diminish from the natural level of the time) and been used as part of a house. The house lasts its full duration and is dismantled. The wood is reused in another house. When that decays, the wood has rotted a bit and

Fig. 25—Radiocarbon sample preparation equipment in Queen's University, Belfast, used to convert the Navan samples into methane.

is re-trimmed to become a piece of furniture that is reused over several generations. Finally, it is accidentally burned in a fire, and its charcoal is used to help date the destruction of the house, that is, the event that finally committed it to the archaeological record. But the wood will give an older date than the event (its burning) that we seek to date. For this and other reasons there is a tendency for ^{14}C dates derived from charcoal to be older than the event they are trying to date. Accordingly, archaeologists are always careful to use charcoal for dating from features where these problems are less likely to arise.

Throughout the excavations Dudley Waterman collected charcoal samples for radiocarbon dating from as many structural features as possible. He was particularly keen to date charcoal from the post-pits and circular foundation slots in the belief that it represented burnt remains of the structures originally built in them. He hoped that the ^{14}C measurements of the samples would not only date the features but also help to confirm the sequence of the archaeological features he had worked out by careful excavation. The age estimation of the Navan samples was carried out in the Radiocarbon Laboratory of Queen's University, Belfast (the UB prefix identifies the processing laboratory as 'University Belfast'). Samples of charcoal from the features to be dated were submitted to the laboratory for dating in several batches over a period of about seven years (Tables 1 and 2).

In 1968 archaeologists were only beginning to gain experience in interpreting dates supplied by laboratories. Broadly speaking, it was believed that the central date quoted by the laboratory was approximately the date of the event being studied. For the reasons explained above, this was unwise. What the laboratory results actually

Table 1—Dates produced for the Navan Fort excavations in October–December 1968.

Sample no.	Description	Age
UB 186	Oak charcoal from the destruction of the large timber building, Phase 5	463±44bc
UB 187	Charcoal from early in Phase 3 (ii), the southern ring-slots	397±50bc
UB 188	Charcoal from the bottom of the Phase 3 (i) ditch	678±50bc
UB 202	Charcoal of small branches from the destruction layer of the large timber building, Phase 4/5	265±50bc
UB 203	Charcoal from the southern enclosure C3, end of Phase 3 (ii)	409±50bc

Table 2—Dates produced for the Navan Fort excavations in December 1970–January 1971.

Sample no.	Description	Age
UB 467	Charcoal from the destruction of the timber building, Phase 5	150±60bc
UB 468	Charcoal from the destruction of the timber building, Phase 5	345±70bc
UB 469	Twigs packed around the central post of the timber building, Phase 4, construction of building	200±70bc
UB 470	Branch in the packing of the central post of the timber building, Phase 4, construction of building	180±65bc

say, for example in the case of UB 203, is that there is a 66% probability that the wood from which the charcoal sample was derived died within the century centred on the radiocarbon date of 409 bc. It is up to the archaeologist to ensure that the charcoal dated is truly representative of the event being dated. A further complication is the need to calibrate the raw dates: to turn them into statistical statements in calendar years.

Looking at the dates above that became available in 1968, Waterman may have tentatively concluded that the early ditch was dug in around 678 BC (UB 188), that Phase 3 (ii) included the year 400 BC (UB 187, UB 203) and that the large timber building burned down in around 265 BC (UB 202). This assessment appears to conform broadly to the finds uncovered and their distribution. The only difficulty was provided by the first Navan date, UB 186, which put the destruction of the timber building back to nearly 500 BC, although this was the most recent event of the series. Perhaps, in the light of the more consistent grouping of the other dates in the expected order of the archaeological layers, this one should be regarded as a 'sport', maybe resulting from the contamination of the sample.

It is clear from the material being submitted to the laboratory that the excavators hoped to use radiocarbon dating to identify, on the one hand, when the building was put up and, on the other, when it was destroyed. This might give an indication of when it stood and for how long. This was a very ambitious plan, given the imprecision inherent in the radiocarbon method and because of potential problems with the origin and age of the sample material. Burnt wood from the destruction of the building could have been put there or died long before the event being dated. Burnt material from the 'destruction layer' may in fact be original material of the building, giving, therefore, further evidence for the date of its construction. Apart from UB 468, which might be regarded as a freak result (perhaps charcoal from an earlier episode was mixed in the sample), the 1970–1 dates for the large timber building appeared to reinforce the 1968 dating of the timber building in broad terms; if anything, they suggested that it may have been even younger, perhaps having been built early in the second century BC.

Results of a further 28 radiocarbon analyses of samples were provided by the Queen's University laboratory between May 1973 and September 1975. Most of the samples were from the figure-of-eight series of conjoined 'southern and northern ring-slots' of Site B and from the 40m structure, either its construction or its destruction. The material dated from the southern ring-slots was mainly charcoal recovered from layers in the slots and believed to be the remains of the structural timbers that had originally been emplaced in the slots (Fig. 26). Since the sequence of slots had been worked out by careful excavation, it was hoped that dating a known sequence of remains of timbers (believed to be parts of the series of buildings) would refine the chronology and indicate broadly which southern and northern enclosures had existed at the same time. The later batches of dates did not greatly alter the picture produced by the first nine. The conventional radiocarbon dates for the 40m structure and Phase 3 (ii–iii), which preceded it, formed two almost-identical series running from around 500 BC to around 100 BC. Not surprisingly, given the reasons stated above, the dates did not conform to the expected order of the structures. Nevertheless, they gave a good indication of the broad period within which the Site B sequence of events took place and suggested that the pre-mound settlement may have existed through the period of the transition from the Late Bronze Age to the Iron Age.

Two dates were obtained from charcoal from the bottom of the Phase 3 (i) ditch, the earliest substantial pre-mound feature, indicating that it had started to silt up in around the seventh century BC. Two dates were obtained for the ring-slots of Site A, Phase A, indicating that they had been filled with burnt material that had died in the period around 200 BC. Phase A of Site A was, therefore, broadly contemporary with the similar features of Phase 3 (ii–iii) nearby at Site B, under the mound. Subsequently, however, the chronology of the site was dramatically refined as a

Fig. 26—Burnt soil and charcoal in one of the Navan Fort ring-slots (Site A, Slot A2).

result of further research carried out by Mike Baillie (see pp 60–1).

Excavation of the sub-mound features was completed in 1970. Several important issues remained to be dealt with by further excavation, particularly the date and nature of the main earthworks and an investigation of the site of a possible entrance. Pressure of other work and worries over what he termed 'the deteriorating political situation' led Waterman to discontinue the excavation and to start restoring the mound in 1971. This was accomplished by hand over a period of several years by some of the workmen who had carried out the excavation.

In the 1970s Waterman prepared a full set of drawings to illustrate his report on the Navan excavations and catalogued the finds. He reorganised the archives and numbering systems for the features in the report in a more user-friendly form. He also wrote an introduction to the report and the descriptive account of the pre-mound features. This proved to be very valuable, as no one else could have satisfactorily sorted out and with first-hand authority described the behaviour of the complex intercutting structural features. During this period I had several conversations with Dudley Waterman about the structure of the report and the interpretation of the structural remains. At the time, this friendly consultation was probably more flattering to me than useful to Waterman, but later the insights thus gained into the structure of the archive and what Waterman thought about what he had uncovered were to prove very valuable. Dudley Waterman died after a short illness in 1979, and in his obituary in the *Ulster Journal of Archaeology* Professor Jope, who had championed his recruitment in 1950, wrote 'It is very sad to realise that his ultimate major work on the interpretation of a decade of excavation at Emain Macha, the ancient capital seat of Uladh at Navan beside Armagh, will now never be presented entirely through his own eye, mind and hand.'

Dún Ailinne

The results of excavations that began on the Hill of Knockaulin in 1968 had a profound influence on the interpretation of the Navan results. Knockaulin, as we have seen, was believed to be one of the other prehistoric legendary provincial capitals of Ireland (Dún Ailinne), with striking similarities to Navan Fort but considerably bigger, averaging 410m in diameter as opposed to Navan's 250m. It is no coincidence that Bernard Wailes of the Department of Anthropology and University Museum, University of Pennsylvania, should have chosen Dún Ailinne at which to carry out research excavations. Bernard was the co-director at Navan in 1963, in charge of the US contingent from the University of Pennsylvania. He was very disappointed at being unable to continue at Navan owing to the withdrawal of funding. The Dún Ailinne excavations proceeded over eight summer seasons between 1968 and 1975.

Dún Ailinne did not have a large summit mound like Navan, but it became clear from the beginning of the excavation on the hilltop that circular trenches were emerging that were very similar to those found under the Site B mound at Navan. These were designated during the dig as the 'Rose' phase and were almost identical on plan to the sub-mound features of Phase 3 (ii) at Navan, initially thought to be 'houses' with attached yards on the north. Similarly, at Dún Ailinne a concentric set of three ring-slot enclosures on the south had east-facing entrances (Fig. 27). They communicated by simple gaps with larger attached enclosures on the north to form a figure-of-eight unit. The northern circles had wide entrances on the east flanked, exactly as at Navan, by a fenced avenue that ran off down the hill to the east towards an entrance through the main outer earthwork. From the discovery of Iron Age material in features that immediately succeeded the 'Rose' phase, it was presumed to date from that period or a little earlier, that is, roughly the same date as similar features were built at Navan. While the nature of the activity represented by the structures remains problematical, the construction of such similar and unusual wooden buildings at two of Ireland's prehistoric sanctuaries at the same time strongly suggested a common purpose in the minds of the designers and builders at the two sites.

The Dún Ailinne structures, however, differed remarkably from the Navan ones in two respects. Firstly, they were much larger: the southern elements were between 15m and 20m in diameter (at Navan they were 10–13.5m), and the attached northern circles were between 27m and 36m in diameter (at Navan they were 20–25m). Secondly, the Dún Ailinne structures lacked any associated occupation material. For these reasons the Dún Ailinne structures were interpreted as having being built for ceremonial purposes. The Navan structures, while rather large for round houses, had been interpreted more prosaically as dwellings for people of high status. But the similarity with the Dún Ailinne structures is such that they were very likely used for the same purpose. Accordingly, Waterman stopped calling the Navan

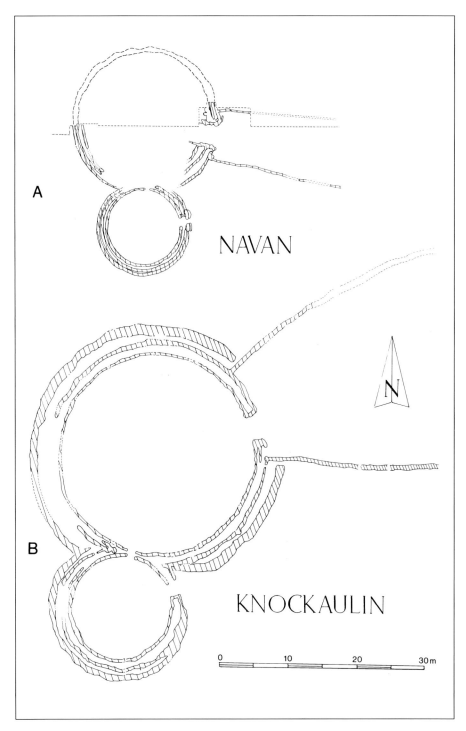

Fig. 27—Plans of the Iron Age figure-of-eight structures at Navan and Knockaulin, Co. Kildare.

Phase 3 figure-of-eight structures 'houses' and changed to the more descriptive and deliberately non-committal terms 'southern ring-slot enclosures' and 'northern ring-slot enclosures' for the joined elements of the figure-of-eight structures. Wailes interpreted the Knockaulin structures as unroofed timber arenas (Fig. 28), while the Navan southern ring-slots were presumed to have been roofed because of their central fireplaces. We will return to the interesting comparisons between the structures found at these two sites as further ideas developed in the course of post-excavation research.

An exotic visitor

In 1976 the animal bones from the Navan excavations were boxed and sent to Ian Hodgson at Duncan of Jordanstone College, Perth, Scotland, for archaeozoological study. Initial scanning of the several thousand fragments of bones as they were being collected and labelled during the dig suggested that they were simply the broken and decayed remains of pigs, cattle and sheep that had been used as food. Bone specialists, however, can identify the species with certainty. They can estimate the age at death and work out the likely number of carcasses represented by the assemblage. They can also identify any peculiarities, such as evidence of disease. If the bones are fairly numerous, their study has much of significance to add to any excavation report; for example, they can tell us whether the community depended

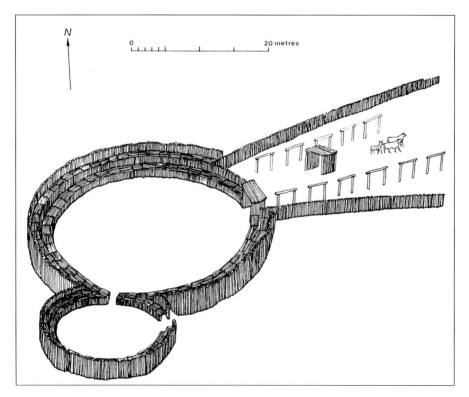

Fig. 28—'Rose' phase structure at Knockaulin interpreted as an unroofed arena.

on beef or dairying, whether there were forests in the vicinity (pigs had to forage for themselves in antiquity), and which environments were exploited for hunting or fishing.

During the study of the animal bones, Hodgson found something very odd: the complete skull of a small animal that had been found in the fill of one of the southern ring-slot enclosures (from C2, part of one of the figure-of-eight foundation trenches, pre-dating the large wooden building). This was unusual, as most bones from the excavation were fragmentary. He did not know what it was and sent it with some other material to Dr J.A. Bateman of the National Museum of Wales. Bateman was clearly intrigued by the skull. He wrote to Waterman to inform him that among the finds from his excavation was the skull of a monkey and that he was sending the specimen to the British Museum, Natural History, for expert confirmation. The skull was positively identified in 1976 as that of a Barbary ape (*Macaque sylvanus*) (Fig. 29). Naturally, Waterman was excited by the news, but he was a little concerned that the object might have been 'planted'. It would be difficult enough, however, to find an ape skull to hoax an excavation with, and there had been no sign at the time of excavation of any interference with the site.

In 1976 the British Museum carried out fluorine tests on the bone to confirm its antiquity. Buried bones absorb fluorine from the soil at a rate that depends on the length of burial. It cannot be used to date bones because the amount absorbed depends on too many variable factors as well as time. All bones, however, buried close together in the same soil at the same time should have equal concentrations of

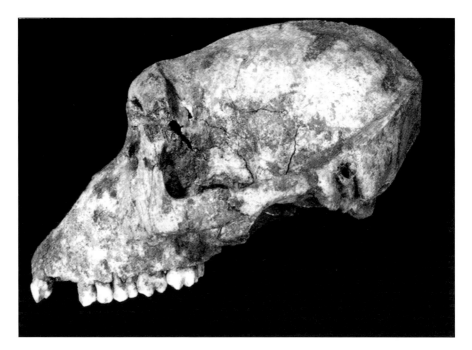

Fig. 29—Skull of a Barbary ape from the Iron Age layers under the Navan mound (photo: British Museum).

fluorine. The Navan ape cranium proved to have the same amount of absorbed fluorine as other bones from the same layer. It could not, therefore, have been planted recently. The matter was fully resolved, however, a few months later when the lower mandible of the same animal was found among a sample of animal bones from another area of the pre-mound excavated surface. More recently, a radiocarbon date was derived from a small sample of collagen from the skull, which was entirely in accord with the time of its context.

More than any other, this find demonstrated the prestige and significance of the site in later prehistory. Today Barbary apes are native in Europe only on the Rock of Gibraltar, but in the past they were to be found only in parts of North Africa. There is some evidence that in classical times there was an organised trade in apes as pets around the Mediterranean. Another specimen has been found in the Tietelberg, an Iron Age hillfort in Luxembourg. Two Roman period sites in Britain have produced incomplete skeletons of Barbary apes. The Navan ape must have been brought from the Mediterranean region, presumably by seafarers or traders. It was a prestige gift to whomever was living on Site B, perhaps given by someone who had acquired the animal from a trader.

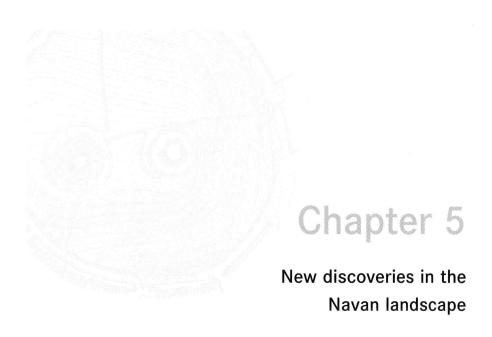

Chapter 5

New discoveries in the Navan landscape

The King's Stables

During my two short spells on the Navan excavations in 1969 and 1970, I had the opportunity to visit and explore interesting sites around Navan and elsewhere in County Armagh, notably the great complex of cross-ridge dykes known as 'the Dorsey' jxust north of Silverbridge. The Dorsey had been connected in legend and folklore with Emain Macha because Dorsey means 'doors' or 'gates' and once it was referred to in medieval annals as the 'Gates of Emain'. Earlier scholars had interpreted the earthworks as some kind of 'frontier post', controlling access to and from an ancient kingdom that had Navan Fort as its capital. In my evening circuit of the Dorsey I had the advantage of having a copy of Harold Tempest's very thorough description of the monument published in the *County Louth Archaeological Journal* of 1930. In 1969 the monument survived much as it did in Tempest's time, but unfortunately several substantial sections have since been levelled.

I also had an opportunity to explore a little around Navan itself and for the first time saw 'the King's Stables'—a peculiar site about 1km west of Navan—and recognised the existence of Haughey's Fort—a large enclosure on a drumlin top 1.5km due west of Navan. We will hear much more of Haughey's Fort, but now, in the unfolding sequence of discovery, it is the turn of the King's Stables to make its contribution to the story of Navan and its landscape.

The King's Stables is an unusual little monument. It survives as a low embankment enclosing all except the southern side of a boggy hollow about 25m in diameter (Fig. 30). The surface of the floating vegetation in the hollow is about 2m below the level of the surrounding farmland. The name may be connected with a local tradition recorded by T.G.F. Paterson that 'the kings of Ulster in the oul' days, watered their horses an' washed their chariots' in the monument. Paterson also

Fig. 30—Aerial view of the King's Stables, a pool surrounded by a bank covered with trees (photo: Mick Aston).

recorded that early in the twentieth century a farmer was discouraged from his attempts to level the monument by the attentions of a ferocious 'dragon' that emerged from the central pool! The date and purpose of this intriguing site were unknown, but there was a suspicion, or rather a hope, that it might in some way be related to Navan.

In August 1975 the Archaeological Survey carried out a trial excavation to obtain some information about the date and purpose of the King's Stables. The landowner had indicated that he wanted to drain or infill the interior as it presented a danger to his livestock, and it was agreed that, if the significance of the site could be demonstrated, another way of dealing with the problem would be found. Before excavation began, duck-boards were laid across the interior of the site and a series of cores were taken across the marshy interior by Jon Pilcher of the Palaeoecology Laboratory, Queen's University, to give some estimate of the depth of the watery hollow and an insight into the nature of the sediments it contained. This showed that the sides of the hollow dropped steeply to a depth of more than 2m and that the bottom was quite flat right across the interior. On the bottom was a thick layer of fine, organic, water-laid mud that must have accumulated in open water; this was covered by about 50cm of fibrous peat, then 50cm of clear water and finally the floating mat of vegetation on which the duck-boards rested. This preview of the layers in the hollow was very promising. It appeared that the King's Stables had indeed been constructed as a regular-sided, flat-bottomed pond that contained standing water from the outset. The fact that over 1m in depth of lake mud had accumulated in the bottom suggested that the monument was of some antiquity, because this material would have built up very slowly. We vaguely hoped that the site might have dated to the time when Navan was in its heyday, the end of the last millennium BC, but were in fact astonished by the actual date when it was revealed by excavation.

The excavation of the King's Stables was confined to a 2m-wide trench running diagonally across the interior from north-west to south-east and continuing across the embankment on that side. The interior of the boggy pond was kept pumped out, and the work would have been impossible had not the late summer of that year been exceptionally dry. As the interior was pumped out, so the 'layer' of water disappeared and the surface level in the monument dropped by as much as 1m. The pump filter was blocked periodically by a mass of aquatic insects drawn into it. They had to be cleared by hand while the pump was kept running. Much water continued to ooze out of the remaining peaty deposits and mud in the sides of the cutting, which was only prevented from moving into the trench by temporary shoring (Fig. 31).

Layers of sandy gravel, perhaps 'wash' from the freshly cut sides and bank of the monument, extended from the edges of the pool into the interior, where they merged with a layer of lake mud 1m deep (identified in the preliminary coring). The lake mud must have settled out of a considerable depth of water over a long time and in itself demonstrated the great age of the site. The gravels at the sides resting on the bottom edge of the pond contained many pieces of hazel and alder twigs that had been cleanly chopped. But the most astonishing finds, which turned up at opposite ends of the diameter examined, were eighteen fragments of moulds of baked clay for casting leaf-shaped bronze swords. There was no way that these finds could have

Fig. 31—Beginning the dig in the waterlogged interior of the King's Stables.

intruded at a later date, so the King's Stables dated from the Late Bronze Age! It was amazing to think that this little pool with its surrounding embankment had survived relatively undisturbed since its construction 3000 years earlier.

The monument, however, had yet more secrets to reveal before the short excavation was completed. Several sherds of coarse pottery, two bone objects, one of them a fine spatula (paralleled elsewhere in Bronze Age sites), and several pieces of smoothed wood completed the artefacts found on the sandstone base of the pool. Most significant, however, were the bones found in the bottom of the pool. During the excavation we were aware that we had found five red deer antlers, the skulls of several dogs and part of a human skull among a more 'normal-looking' collection of domesticated species. After the excavation Christine Penn identified 214 animal bones to species: 36% cattle, 31% dog, 20% pig, 9% red deer, 3% sheep, 1% 'other' (horse, badger and 'indeterminate'). This is a small sample on which to base general conclusions, but even these bones had some strange aspects. For example, some of the dog bones appear to have come from intact skeletons, suggesting that the animals had been deposited complete or had died at or in the pool. The sizes and laterality of the antlers suggested that they had come from five different deer, and four of them had been broken off the skulls of dead animals. The human skull fragment was found on the sandstone floor of the pool near the centre (Fig. 32). It was the facial portion of the skull of a young adult male (excluding the mandible), which showed signs of having been deliberately detached in antiquity from the rest of the skull. In contrast to the contemporary animal bones, it was relatively poorly preserved, perhaps having been kept for some time in a peaty (acidic) environment.

It seems reasonable to conclude that the King's Stables was an artificial pool. It had held deep water from the time of its construction. Three radiocarbon analyses carried out on twigs from the bottom of the pond suggest that this took place around 1000 BC. The presence of the sword moulds, the strange collection of animal bones and the human skull fragment all point to a ritual or ceremonial function for this enigmatic artificial pool. The King's Stables may well have been built even before the construction of the Phase 3 (i) (Late Bronze Age) ditch under the Site B mound in Navan Fort. Records of the sites of two destroyed cairns in Ballybrolly townland, 1km to the north of Navan Fort, testify to the use of the immediate landscape from as long ago as the Neolithic period, perhaps around 2500 BC. But the excavation of the King's Stables, a Bronze Age ceremonial monument, and at the same time the identification of Haughey's Fort nearby as a likely prehistoric hillfort led to the recognition that we could be dealing with a complex of related sites. This would now be termed an 'archaeological landscape', even though many of the monuments had been almost levelled. The sites were of different dates and purposes, but the position and function of later monuments may have been determined to an extent by the earlier ones. The monuments testified to continuity in the way the area was perceived and used by successive communities over a long period of time.[*]

[*]The King's Stables was later acquired by the Department of the Environment to secure its protection.

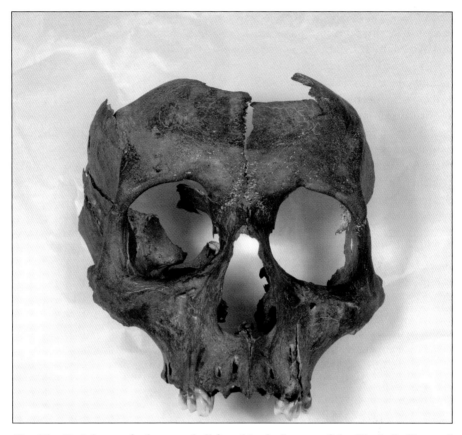

Fig. 32—Facial part of a human skull found in the bottom of the King's Stables pool.

The Dorsey

I have tried to explain the discovery of most of the insights into Navan and related monuments in the appropriate sequence in time, but this is not always logical or possible. Some of the other sites and issues involved have long histories of investigation, and a narrative that was rigid in chronology would tell ten stories at once, constantly leaping from place to place. Now, however, seems to be the right time to mention the Dorsey, as this separate story leads up to the moment in the early 1980s when tree-ring dating of timbers found in excavations at these earthworks provided a dramatic insight into the dating of Navan Fort and related monuments.

South and east of Navan the undulating landscape rises gently to the hills of southern County Armagh, beyond which lies the plain of north Louth, the ancient Mag Muirtheimne. Several passes between natural barriers such as rocky hills (anciently known as Sliab Fuait), lakes and bogs provide natural lines of communication between the fertile plains of Armagh and Louth. The central pass in this area, on a line between Dundalk, Co. Louth, and Newtownhamilton, Co. Armagh, is straddled by a series of large banks and ditches known as 'the Dorsey', just north of Silverbridge. The main earthwork, a large bank with a deep ditch on either side, is 700m long and crosses two parallel ridges at a point where they are traversed by an ancient routeway. Traces of a smaller, and arguably earlier, bank lie some 300m to the north, giving the monument the appearance of a large irregular enclosure encompassing hills, bogs and pasture. The whole circuit of the monument cannot be seen from any single vantage point (Fig. 33).

The Dorsey was fully described in 1930 by Henry G. Tempest, a Dundalk publisher and archaeologist. He republished early maps, descriptions and local traditions. The monument has often been linked to Navan. For example, the Annals of Clonmacnoise appear to refer to the place in AD 1224 as *doirsiu Emna*, that is, the 'doors/gates of Emain'. Tempest concluded that the Dorsey was 'a fortified frontier post of the Kingdom whose capital was Emain Macha', blocking an important historical route or pass into southern Armagh and built at a time when the Ulaidh's power was strongest. Sometime later, according to Tempest, the Ulaidh were threatened from the south, and they may have incorporated the Dorsey into a defence system of separate and relatively short lengths of embankment running across Ireland, known in some places as the 'Black Pig's Dyke' and in others as the 'Worm Ditch'. Although these lengths of earthwork are widely separated, they have similar profiles, and where excavations have taken place they have been shown to date from the Early Iron Age (Fig. 34).

A series of small excavations at the Dorsey was sponsored by the Ancient Monuments Advisory Council (Northern Ireland) in the late 1930s. In the first of these, Oliver Davies found that the eastern gap through which the 'old coach road'

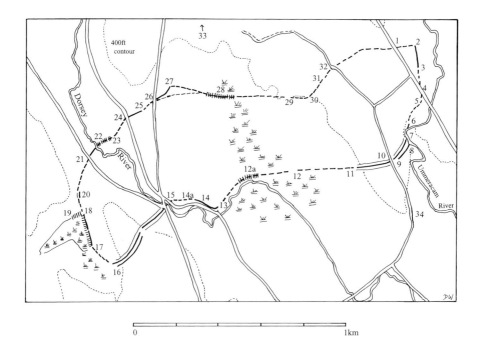

Fig. 33—Plan of the Dorsey based on H.G. Tempest's study.

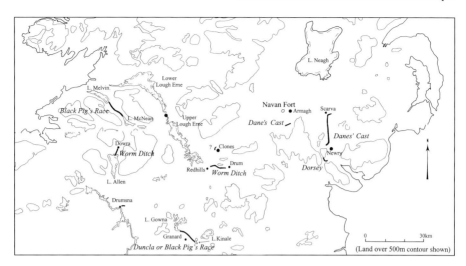

Fig. 34—Map showing sections of linear earthworks in the north of Ireland.

runs is an original feature (Fig. 33, points 9 and 10). This proved that the earthworks were designed not to block the route completely but perhaps to channel access through defined gaps, possibly the 'doors' or 'gates' of the place-name. On the eastern side of this gap, Davies reported the discovery of lines of post-holes, stone settings and small trenches, suggesting the presence of early, but undated, habitation, perhaps a 'guardhouse'.

In another excavation in 1938 Davies examined the western end of the Dorsey and found some evidence for his suggestion that another earthwork, which he called the 'Black Pig's Dyke', joined the Dorsey on the west side and that the two structures were of the same age (Fig. 33, point 19). The most interesting discovery in this early series of excavations on the south-west was a 'row of oak piles and side-pieces' in boggy ground immediately east of the former line of the earthwork where it had been levelled by a landowner (Fig. 33, point 17). While Davies' excavations in the late 1930s added some details to Tempest's account with respect to the original scale, position and character of the earthworks, they provided no new evidence for the date and function of the monument. At that time, dating of sites depended on the discovery of datable artefacts that could be related confidently to the structure in question (earlier, later or contemporaneous). Davies did not find any diagnostic artefacts, and of course dendrochronology and radiocarbon dating were not available. His final conclusion, a variation of Tempest's theory, was that the Dorsey was in some way linked to Emain Macha, that it was part of the Black Pig's Dyke system and that it may have been used by the Ulaidh as a 'temporary kraal' into which herds of cattle, perhaps looted from the south, could be driven and defended, pending distribution among their captors. A further 38 years elapsed before another opportunity arose for an investigation of the Dorsey.

In 1977 a layer of charcoal was exposed accidentally under the bank of the smaller, northern section of the earthwork at the eastern end (Fig. 33, point 31). This was subsequently shown by a trial excavation to derive from the burning of timbers or brushwood immediately before the bank was heaped over their smouldering remains (Fig. 35). The charcoal was radiocarbon dated, demonstrating that the timbers were felled in the Early Iron Age, probably somewhere between 400 BC and 1 BC. Even more dramatically, the row of oak timbers over 1km away at the west, noted earlier by both Tempest and Davies, was by chance revealed during bulldozing at the same time as the excavation of the burnt layer on the east. We discovered this by accident one evening when the excavation team decided to explore the circuit of the monument (Fig. 33, points 16–17). The timbers were excavated hurriedly and interpreted as the stumps of uprights for a wooden palisade running parallel to the line of the rampart, which was reduced in size here where it flanked the bog on the west. Several of the close-packed oak post-butts and split-plank side-pieces were removed and studied in the Palaeoecology Centre, Queen's University, Belfast, by Mike Baillie and Dave Brown to see if they could be used in completing the construction of a tree-ring chronology for Ireland and whether the felling of the timbers could be dated in calendar years (Fig. 36).

Dating the Navan mound

Oak trees put on a single growth ring every year. The width of the ring varies according to the climatic factors in that year. The result is that, as you look at a slice extracted from an oak growing today and count back 200 rings from the outside toward the centre, you know that the tree grew that particular inner ring on its *outside* two centuries ago. The same is true for every other oak. Not only that, within the north of Ireland the pattern of the rings (changes in ring widths, groups of wide

Fig. 35—Gully and burnt material found under the bank of the Dorsey on the north-east (north is to the left).

Fig. 36—Oak post-bases and side-pieces uncovered at the western end of the Dorsey in 1977.

and narrow rings) through the two centuries will be identical. This is because all of the oaks were subject to the same vagaries of climate in the same region and all react in the same way. Thus dendrochronologists can work backwards in time, matching overlapping ring patterns using timbers from a variety of places—trees, buildings, archaeological sites and bogs—to set up a standard pattern of tree-ring widths stretching back from the present into prehistory (a 'master chronology'). At no point in the sequence does the pattern repeat itself, because annual climatic changes never repeat in a long pattern. The result is that, in theory, any piece of oak that has preserved a sequence of 100 or more measurable tree-rings can be dated by comparing its pattern with that on the 'master chronology' (Fig. 37). Naturally, the matching is done by computer. Some specimens of timber for dating come from the core of the tree, in which case the closest we can get to the date of felling is the year in which the most recent preserved ring of the specimen grew. The archaeologist, however, hopes to have bark or even the outer rings near the bark (sapwood) on the sample in order to know the decade or even the year in which the tree was felled or the branch was cut off.

In the 1970s, just after the Navan excavation was completed, Mike Baillie constructed a Navan tree-ring chronology, spanning 192 years, from the remains of the excavated oak timbers at the site, mainly the large central post (it was not tied down to calendar years). This chronology 'floated' in time, as the master chronology had not at that time been extended from the present back into the Iron Age. By 1980 the 'Belfast tree-ring chronology' extended back to 13 BC. There was then a gap to about 200 BC (dated by correlation with tree-ring sequences in Britain), after which the Belfast chronology stretched back to around 5000 BC.

The timbers recovered from the palisade at the western end of the Dorsey yielded a 246-year-long tree-ring sequence that completely matched the 192-year-long Navan sequence. This unique 'Navan–Dorsey chronology' not only tied into the master chronology but also formed an important link in establishing the overall 7272-year-long Irish tree-ring chronology. In 1986 Mike Baillie published the news that the Navan–Dorsey chronology covered the period 316 BC to 116 BC.

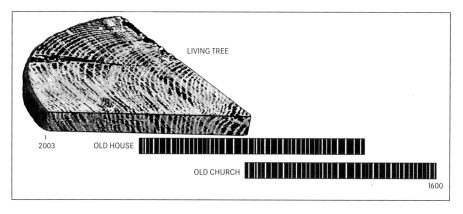

LIVING TREE

2003   OLD HOUSE

OLD CHURCH

1600

Fig. 37—Diagram showing how tree-ring patterns can be matched backwards from the present.

Allowance for missing sapwood (the softer, living, outer rings on the trees) suggested that both sets of timbers were felled in around 100 BC. Later, in 1987, it was possible to re-examine the Navan central post in its conservation tank in Moira, Co. Down. This revealed that complete sapwood survived in a narrow indentation on the post right out to the under-bark surface. As a result, the timber was re-sectioned across this hollow, and the sapwood rings were counted and re-matched to the master chronology *This showed that the oak tree used as the central feature of the Navan timber structure last grew in 95 BC.* It was felled either in that year or early in 94 BC. The Dorsey was probably built, or perhaps was re-fortified, in the same decade, 100–91 BC.

This accurate dating of both sites strongly supports earlier suggestions that the Dorsey and Navan Fort (Emain Macha) were in some way connected and proved that the monuments dated from the Early Iron Age. The exercise also showed that the Dorsey earthworks were accompanied by a number of timber structures and palisades of considerable scale and of different dates, earlier than the smaller embankment on the north and presumably contemporaneous with the large earthwork on the south.

In 1982 a section was cut by Aidan Walsh of Monaghan County Museum through a part of the Black Pig's Dyke near Scotshouse, Co. Monaghan. Here, too, remains of a palisade, this time burnt, were found running parallel to the earthworks. Radiocarbon dates from the charcoal show that the palisade, and presumably the earthwork, was also erected in the Early Iron Age. Close similarities in the siting, profile and date between this piece of the Dyke and the southern sections of the Dorsey suggest that the two may have been closely related. Perhaps they were parts of a brief phase of construction of earthwork and timber defences, blocking routeways separated by natural obstacles.

The Dorsey as a series of earthworks
More recently a suggestion has been made that the Dorsey is not a single earthwork built at one time. It may comprise two sets of cross-ridge dykes, the smaller, northern earthworks being earlier (Fig. 33, points 18–2). The larger, southern earthworks (Fig. 33, points 2–16) may represent a strengthening of the defences in the pass added to the earlier work in such a way as to create not so much an enclosure as two lines of defences with protection on the flanks. This suggestion is supported by the accidental discovery by Pat Loye in 1988 of a dump of large axe-marked oak timbers in the ditch of the northern section of the Dorsey at point 25 (Fig. 33). Most of the timbers of this group that were dated using dendrochronology by Mike Baillie and Dave Brown were felled in the 140s BC or earlier. If the evidence is taken at face value, it suggests that the northern section of the earthwork was built around 40 years before the much larger, southern sections. This sequence could be altered if, for example, the palisade uncovered at points 16–17 had been added to the southern rampart long after its original construction, or if the oak stumps found in 1988 at point 25 had been lying around for a long time before being rolled into a newly cut ditch (unlikely). There is also a possibility that the southern earthworks are not of one period: remains of an earlier defensive work on this line may have

been buried under its banks or cut away by its ditches. At least, however, the fact that the Dorsey is a complex of earthwork and timber defences, with different phases of construction, seems firmly established.

Since these relatively widely separated monuments, the mound in Navan Fort and the Dorsey, seem to be related, it is perhaps worth observing that, conceptually at least, the Dorsey and perhaps some other isolated stretches of dykes should be considered as potentially outlying parts of the 'Navan Complex'. Since Navan Fort was apparently used as a sanctuary in the Iron Age, with clear archaeological evidence for ceremonial activity in around 100 BC and earlier, it is possible that the Dorsey also had a significant religious function, perhaps defining the limit of a sacred core territory rather than providing a boundary that could be defended militarily. Other monument complexes in Ireland that seem to have had significance in later prehistory also have unusual curvilinear embankments, for example the Knockans at Teltown, Co. Meath (recently excavated by Professor Waddell of University College Galway), and the Mucklaghs of Rath Croghan, Co. Roscommon.

If, as suggested here, the major phases of earthwork and timber construction in the 90s BC at Dorsey and Navan were closely 'related', maybe even built by the same people, a possibility arises that phases of activity or construction at both sites immediately preceding the 90s BC were similarly 'related'. The most recently published speculation on the purpose of the Dorsey was offered by Nick Aitchison in 1993. He extensively reviewed earlier research and interpretations of the site and suggested that the Dorsey was associated with ritual activity, that it was a 'sacred' enclosure, that the Dorsey and Navan Fort may have fulfilled similar functions, and that they may have belonged to 'two different socio-political groups, tramontane peoples whose principal ritual centres lay on opposite sides of the Fews' (a barony name derived from Sliab Fuait, the low mountain of south Armagh). Aitchison is correct, I believe, in pointing out the potential ritual significance of the site. I would suggest, however, that the ritual significance of the Dorsey arose mainly from its relation to Navan Fort (Emain Macha) rather than from the Dorsey constituting a ritual centre in its own right, independent of Emain Macha. Aitchison writes that 'the constituent elements of the Dorsey may be recognised in other Iron Age sites such as Navan Fort, *Ráth na Ríogh* at Tara, Knockaulin and the Dun of Drumsna'. Yes to banks, ditches and palisades, but the layout and positioning of the Dorsey are unlike the other monuments cited.

Thanks to the application of laboratory dating techniques in Queen's University, Belfast, we now have more accurate knowledge of the date and development of the Dorsey than would have been dreamed possible by Tempest. The Dorsey remains enigmatic in many ways, but much useful information still survives in the ground and will be revealed in future excavations.

The quarry

While working at Navan Site B on the excavation of the pre-mound surface in 1970, I stayed behind one evening to help Dudley Waterman complete some recording so that excavation of the features in question could continue the next day. As we were walking from the site office onto the excavation, we suddenly found ourselves thrown to the ground by a fierce earth tremor. I thought for a moment that the end of the world had arrived. The thought only lasted a moment because within a second of being thrown down we heard an enormous explosion from the limestone quarry only 150m to the east. From my recumbent position I recall seeing huge pieces of rock fired up into the air and spinning in slow motion like cinema asteroids. Several of them plugged deep into the ground within Navan Fort itself.

The earliest mention of quarrying at Navan (by implication) is in AD 1145, when the Annals of the Four Masters note that 'A lime-kiln, which was sixty feet every way, was erected opposite Emain Macha by Gillamacliag, successor of Patrick, and Patrick's clergy in general'. Perhaps this was to make mortar for a major phase of ecclesiastical building in Armagh, which could also have derived stone from the area. In more recent times, however, much of the limestone from which public buildings in Armagh were constructed seems to have come from a quarry in the vicinity of Navan. In the 1960s Armagh was occasionally rocked late on Friday afternoons by blasts from the Navan quarry. By the time the excavations at Navan were well under way in the late 1960s, the deep limestone quarry had extended northward from Navan Fort Road for some 350m, effectively cutting off Navan from Loughnashade, an integral part of the archaeological landscape.

In the summer of 1969 large earth-moving machines arrived and scraped off some 10m of boulder clay overburden over a long stretch of the hillside immediately east of the Fort. The subsequent blasting and quarrying of the rock thus exposed created an enormous pit between the Fort and Loughnashade (Fig. 38). The

Fig. 38—The quarry and industrial site between Navan, centre left, and Loughnashade, right, looking west.

landscape was further damaged by the piling up of the quarry spoil in a large dump on the eastern side of the quarry, partly spilling into the margin of Loughnashade. While regretting the damage to this unique landscape caused by the quarry, the Ancient Monuments Branch of the Ministry of Finance (which ran the excavation on the Fort) was powerless to do anything about the quarry expansion, probably feeling fortunate to have secured the preservation of the monument itself. At that time the significance of archaeological landscapes had not been clearly articulated, and large-scale rescue excavation of superficially blank fields was not contemplated. In truth, it is not possible to say what remains of significance were removed by the quarry. Waterman's own opinion is noted in the introduction to his report on the excavations written in 1978, where he recorded that the Fort was acquired for the state by compulsory purchase in the same year and that 'The amenities of the site, however, have been, and continue to be, threatened by the working of an adjacent limestone quarry'.

The problem was that in those days extant quarries did not require planning permission. In the early 1980s new regulations required that quarries should apply for planning permission to expand. At Navan the quarry had acquired farmland on the south and north that, if worked, would have left the monument surrounded by a cliff beneath its outer edge on all sides except the west. An application to extend the quarry to the north was the subject of a planning inquiry in 1985.

In the period leading up to the inquiry archaeologists and officials working for the Department of the Environment, which managed Navan Fort but which was also the planning authority, were obliged to refrain from public comment on the case. Other archaeologists, however, notably Jim Mallory and Tom McNeill of Queen's University and Richard Warner of the Ulster Museum, set up a pressure group known as the 'Friends of Navan'. As a result of media opportunities, publications and a busy round of evening public lectures and debates, the Friends of Navan managed to organise and focus public support for the preservation of the monument and its landscape setting. This was demonstrated by the volume of letters opposed to the quarry sent to the inquiry and by the number and quality of the objectors heard in the inquiry. Not only did this help in opposition to the quarry but it also raised public awareness in Ireland and elsewhere of the significance of Navan, its archaeology and associated legendary material. The inquiry found in favour of the quarry extension, but this decision was overturned by the Minister for the Environment, Richard Needham. As a result, quarrying at Navan ceased in 1987. The vast quarry pit at Navan (now filled with blue water) has had to be screened from the monument by a 2m high wall to prevent visitors to the site from straying over the edge.

Chapter 6

Bigger and older:
Haughey's Fort and the Navan Complex

Attention was drawn to the potential significance of Haughey's Fort when the excavations of the King's Stables were published and the concept of a wider landscape complex of Navan-related monuments began to take shape. In 1986 the Navan Research Group was set up jointly by the Department of the Environment, Queen's University, Belfast, and the Ulster Museum to pursue archaeological research into Navan and its landscape. It was agreed to publish the results of the research, which included, literary, historical and mythological material, in *Emania*, the bulletin of the Navan Research Group. *Emania* first appeared in 1986, and its nineteenth issue has been published. From 1986 onwards the story of Navan research is comprehensively told in *Emania*. Jim Mallory is editor of the bulletin and, with his background in both archaeology and linguistics, is perhaps the only person capable of covering with authority both the archaeological and the literary aspects of research connected with Navan and the Iron Age in general.

After the ministerial decision to halt quarrying in 1986 and the setting up of the Navan Research Group, Mallory began to consider the possibility of finding time to become directly involved in archaeological fieldwork in the Navan area. This also provided a suitable opportunity for introducing university students and others to the techniques of fieldwork and excavation. The King's Stables had been examined; there was a moratorium on further digging in Navan; and the destroyed Ballybrolly megalith sites were inaccessible. Attention therefore focused on Haughey's Fort, at that time the only other potentially significant monument known in the immediate area. Haughey's Fort and the hill on which it stands were ploughed in the spring of 1987, and I arranged to fieldwalk it with Jim Mallory and Jackie McDowell, who was at that time directing excavations on early ecclesiastical sites in Armagh City. We found some sherds of pottery and flint scrapers consistent with a Bronze Age date, and an exposure of red-burnt soil and charcoal in some of the deeper furrows was a good indication that significant archaeological features survived. With the generous consent of the landowner, Mrs H. Morton, and the tenant farmer, Mr Noel Greer, Mallory began excavation in Haughey's Fort in the summer of 1987.

Haughey's Fort stands on a hill in Tray townland approximately 1km west of Navan Fort. When one stands in Haughey's Fort and looks east, the Navan mound appears to sit on top of the intervening hill in Creeveroe. It is marked as a monument only on the second edition (1858) of the 6-inch-scale Ordnance Survey map (Armagh, sheet 12), which depicts the outline of an oval enclosure, 150m in diameter, described as the 'site of fort'. The modern name of the site comes from the farmer who worked the land in the nineteenth century. It consists essentially of modern field boundaries following, for the most part, the inner edge of what appeared to be a large, silted-up ditch (Fig. 39). Several seasons of excavation were carried out in Haughey's Fort from 1987 to 1995, which resulted in a rich stream of some twenty articles in *Emania* dealing with the excavations and specialist studies on the finds, as well as environmental evidence such as animal bones, waterlogged wood and pottery. Altogether, about 10 per cent of the area within the hilltop enclosure has been excavated, so a considerable amount of archaeological material remains to be protected for future research.

The excavations showed that Haughey's Fort was occupied in the Late Bronze Age, roughly between 1100 and 900 BC, contemporaneously with the King's Stables. The results of an aerial photographic survey, published by Barrie Hartwell in 1991, showed that Haughey's Fort had two outer concentric ditches with a

Fig. 39—Haughey's Fort from the south, showing the excavation trench in the centre and an outer ditch as a cropmark in the field to the north (photo: Queen's University, Belfast).

maximum overall diameter of some 350m. Haughey's Fort is, therefore, larger than Navan Fort and is a millennium older than the Site B mound. The larger, inner ditch enclosed an area 150m across and contained a series of concentric arcs of pits of various sizes (Fig. 40). The large pits produced Late Bronze Age pottery, tiny fragments of gold ornaments, carbonised seeds, and burnt and unburnt animal bone. Some of the post-holes may have formed the outline of an enclosure or stockade, the relationships of which to other excavated features and to the earthworks of the fort itself are not clear. From pottery and other material disposed of in the features, it is clear that much of the occupation and perhaps ceremonial activity in Haughey's Fort dates from the Late Bronze Age.

A long section of the inner ditch was excavated on the south-east side of the enclosure. This was waterlogged at the base and produced a large quantity of animal bones, pieces of wood (including an axe handle), seeds, insect remains and pottery (Fig. 41). The ditch bottom was 2.8m below the present ground surface. The animal bones recovered from the pits and from the inner ditch indicate that the livestock of the Bronze Age people consisted of cattle and pig, but there were also some bones of dog and sheep/goat. Wild mammal remains were few and included pig, red deer and fox. Some of the skulls of the domesticated animals were unusually large for the period, but two dog skulls found in the ditch were the largest from any prehistoric site in Ireland. Some have joked that these were the ancestors of Cullain's fierce hound, from which the hero of Emain Macha, Cú Chulainn, got his name.

The excavations at Haughey's Fort have amounted to a small industry, and a generation of archaeology undergraduates discovered the techniques of excavation on this County Armagh drumlin. Some went on to develop theses and publications on the basis of the excavated material. Jim Mallory and his team have demonstrated the archaeological significance of the site; the large Bronze Age hillfort accords with a pattern emerging elsewhere and, in terms of finds and material for environmental studies, is one of the most prolific sites of its type yet to have been excavated in Ireland. Several fundamental questions have been raised by the excavations at Haughey's Fort, which future research may try to answer. It has been generally concluded from the pottery, the size and number of the animal bones, and the presence of small gold ornaments that Haughey's Fort may have been the general focus of settlement with an aristocratic component in the early part of the Late Bronze Age. It is not clear whether the multiple ditches were purely for defence or had a religious function as well. Perhaps it is safest to keep all possibilities open for the present. The same applies to the internal structures on the top of the hill: are the pits ritual or domestic, or both? The discovery of a cup-and-ring marked stone in the excavation on the hilltop suggests a religious dimension. Cup-and-ring marked stones are found along the Atlantic coasts of north-west Europe and are thought to be mandala-like symbols dating from the Neolithic or the Early Bronze Age. It has been suggested that the cup-and-ring marked boulder found in Haughey's Fort was brought there from elsewhere and was reburied as a 'votive' deposit (Fig. 42).

Does the discovery of a curving fence indicate the separation of a special area in Haughey's Fort, and how does it relate to the earthwork? It cannot always be

Fig. 40—Concentric arcs of post- and stake-holes at the centre of Haughey's Fort (photo: Queen's University, Belfast).

Fig. 41—Excavated stretch of the inner ditch of Haughey's Fort on the south-east (photo: Queen's University, Belfast).

Fig. 42—Cup-and-ring marked stone uncovered in Haughey's Fort (photo: Queen's University, Belfast).

assumed that archaeological features found within a monument or an enclosed space are contemporary with one another or with the enclosure. Most significantly in the present context we must ask: what role did Haughey's Fort and its inhabitants have in the siting, purpose and construction of the mound in Navan Fort in the first century BC? Several pits in the interior, however, did produce Iron Age finds, suggesting that Haughey's Fort may have been occupied for nearly a thousand years or, more likely, that it was reoccupied in the Iron Age. There was no evidence for a major refurbishment of the Bronze Age earthworks in the Iron Age. Sherds of a type of coarse cooking pottery known as 'souterrain ware', dating from the Early Christian period, around AD 900, were found in the middle ditch and show that the feature had by then silted up to within 70cm of the present ground surface. They do not show, however, that Haughey's Fort as such was reoccupied at this time. Although the outer defences of the fort may have been more prominent in the Iron Age, it is possible that the features and finds dating from this period were found on any drumlin top in the area and that their depositors were making use of the old hillfort only because it was convenient to do so. We cannot argue that Haughey's Fort was in some way 'ancestral' to Navan Fort, the date of which was assumed to be Iron Age at this time only because of the date of the Site B mound. But the construction of such a prestige monument in the Bronze Age gives the monumental Navan landscape added breadth and depth. The wider area around Haughey's Fort, including the drumlin that was later to become Navan Fort, must have been viewed as valuable—economically, socially and spiritually—throughout prehistory. (The entire extent of Haughey's Fort is scheduled for protection under the Historic Monuments and Archaeological Objects Order (Nothern Ireland), 1995, and the central area of some 4 acres (1.5ha) enclosed by the inner bank was purchased by the Department of the Environment in 2003.)

Loughnashade and its contents

In 1987 *Emania* published two early accounts of the discovery of the Loughnashade trumpets, or horns, the first by Arthur Browne, a fellow of Trinity College, Dublin, and printed in the *Transactions* of the Royal Irish Academy in 1802:

> Being at Armagh in September last, I was casually informed that one of the tenants of his grace the Primate, by name Pooler, had in his possession some ancient trumpets not so long since dug out of a neighbouring bog. I went to his house and there saw two of them, and afterwards a third at the house of an artist in Armagh, where it had been sent to be repaired: a drawing of the most perfect is hereunto annexed.

> Mr Pooler informed me, that four of them had been dug up at the same time, and nearly in the same place; and that the tradition of the place is, that a mighty battle was there once fought, and that some King of Ulster had his palace not far distant; but when, or between whom the combat was reported to have been, he could not give me any information.

Their antiquity appears from the peculiarity of the metallic composition, which is different from any of the modern times; and from the parts being joined entirely by rivets, evidently before the art of soldering was known; and from the ornaments about the entire, I think it plain that they must have appertained to a nation not in a state of barbarism. When I saw them they were not sufficiently in repair or tight to produce sound; but one of them has been made by an artist, in the vulgar expression, wind-tight, and sounded by a trumpeter belonging to the 23rd Regiment of Dragoons, and, as I was informed, produced a tremendous sound, which could be heard for miles.

In his *Historical memoir of the City of Armagh*, published in 1819, James Stuart recorded that:

In the year 1798, four brazen trumpets were found in boggy land, on the borders of Loughnashade, near Armagh, in the property of Robert Pooler, of Tyross, Esq...The trumpets...are of a golden colour, and nearly similar in size, form and structure. One of these, now in the possession of Mr Pooler himself, consists of two joints—the length of the whole sweep, which is nearly semicircular, is six feet...One of these curious trumpets was presented by Mr Pooler to Lieutenant-General Alexander Campbell, and by him removed to Scotland. The second was given to Colonel Hall of Armagh. The third was purloined; the fourth and most imperfect of the whole, is the one now in possession of Mr Pooler.

Near the trumpets, were found human skulls and other bones, which, by the antiseptic quality of the bog, had been preserved uninjured, though their colour had been changed to a dusky brown. We have seen one of these skulls in the possession of John Simpson, Esq., M.D.

The whereabouts of three of the trumpets are now unknown, but the fourth is in the National Museum of Ireland, Dublin. Professor Barry Raftery pointed out that finds of such great curved instruments of sheet bronze are rare and seem to be an essentially Irish development. The only surviving comparable specimen was found in 1809 in 'peat moss' at Ardbrin, Co. Down. The finder, as soon as he had cleared the tube of the moss it contained, blew a blast 'which immediately arrested the attention of the inhabitants of several adjacent townlands, who hurried to the spot'. A fragment of a similar horn was found among a large deposit of Iron Age metalwork discovered in a bog at Llyn Cerrig Bach on Anglesea, northern Wales, in 1940.

As Raftery pointed out, the making of a horn such as that from Loughnashade represents a spectacular feat of craftsmanship. The bronze sheets had first to be bent and hammered around a long mandrel, or pre-shaped core. An internal sealing strip was then inserted. Rivet-holes were then drilled through the two thicknesses of metal, and the core was removed. Very long tweezers were then used to insert flat-headed rivets into the holes from the inside. The mandrel, or mould, was reinserted, and the rivets were hammered flat and then filed smooth. Finally the tubes were bent to the desired form, perhaps by applying heat and pressure after they had been

Fig. 43—Bronze disc decorated in La Tène style forming the bell end of the horn from Loughnashade, first century BC/AD (photo: National Museum of Ireland).

temporarily filled with sand and sealed to prevent buckling.

The bell end of the surviving horn in the National Museum of Ireland is a disc of bronze, finely decorated in a *repoussé* technique (hammered or punched up from behind) with La Tène-style swirling ornament (Fig. 43). The attachment securing this in place is modern and is assumed to be correct. It has been suggested, however, that the disc is not part of the horn and may be a fitting from some other object.

The care and attention lavished on the horns make it clear that they were used for some extraordinary purpose on occasions of special significance. Raftery suggests that they were blown during processions or religious ceremonies or in the course of military confrontations. He quotes Polybius's account of the battle of Telamon fought between the Gauls and the Romans in 225 BC:

> The Romans were terrified by the fine order of the Celtic host, and the dreadful din, for there were innumerable hornblowers and trumpeters and, as the whole army were shouting their war-cries at the same time, there was such a tumult of sound that not only the trumpets and the soldiers but all the country round had got a voice and caught up the cry.

The four horns in Loughnashade were not lost accidentally, and it is unlikely that they were hidden with the intention of recovery. The most likely explanation is that they were deposited as an offering in the context of a religious ceremony. The discovery of human remains nearby during the same digging may reinforce the votive explanation for the presence of these magnificent objects, although the human remains may not be contemporaneous with the horns. The fragment of a similar horn from Anglesea must have been deposited before about AD 60, when the Romans destroyed the sanctuaries on the island. The disc on the end of the surviving Loughnashade horn could have been made a century either side of the birth of Christ. It is difficult to avoid the conclusion that there was a connection between Loughnashade ('the Lake of the Treasures') and Navan Fort, the sanctuary that overlooks it. Both sites were used for ceremonial purposes in the Iron Age, and there is nothing comparable elsewhere in the region. We cannot, however, at this stage equate individual episodes at the two sites, for example horn deposition with mound construction. The 90s BC would be at the earliest limit of the date range for the decoration on the trumpet end-piece. While the natural lake and the nearby hill and artificial enclosure may have been perceived as significant parts of a sanctuary complex, there is no reason to presume that activity in one part must have been matched by some related ceremonial in the other. Nevertheless, the horns are very significant in their own right, and Loughnashade would be famous for their discovery even if Navan Fort and the rest of the complex did not exist. This renders all the more regrettable the presence of the vast quarry hole and spoilheaps that now separate Navan from the lake and that have altered the landscape of the area immediately east of the fort.

Loughnashade was at least four times greater in extent in 1835 than it is today. Perhaps it was in the peaty margins of this larger lake that the horns were found during drainage in 1798. In any event, because of the discovery of the Iron Age horns in or near the lake, it and an area around it have been scheduled for protection under the Historic Monuments and Archaeological Objects Order (Northern Ireland), 1995.

The Navan Complex

Several writers have contributed interesting papers to *Emania* on the sites and finds in the Navan landscape that have been identified as constituting the 'Navan Complex'. Richard Warner of the Ulster Museum has studied neighbouring sites and mapped earlier finds of archaeological material in the vicinity; Barrie Hartwell has carried out and published aerial photographic surveys; and Jim Mallory has looked at the 'literary topography' of Navan and assessed whether the places monitored in the tales and early literature can be matched with the site and monuments as they survive today.

The Navan Complex is a palimpsest of ploughed-down earthwork monuments dating from the Neolithic period, around 3000 BC, to the modern field system, with every period in between being well represented (Fig. 44). The oldest features are, of course, the natural landscape itself—hills, lakes, streams and bogs—which forms the background on which successive generations left their marks.

Fig. 44—The Navan area from the air looking north. Navan Fort and Loughnashade
are on the right; Haughey's Fort and the King's Stables are to the left.

Monuments

The first edition of the Ordnance Survey 6-inch-scale map shows the sites of two
stone circles, probably the remains of Neolithic passage tombs, in Ballybrolly
townland, 1km to the north of Navan. One of these survived until the 1960s but was
progressively destroyed during the construction of farm outbuildings over a number
of years. Haughey's Fort, as we have seen, is a major Bronze Age monument 1km
west of Navan, and aerial photography in 1989 revealed the presence and great
extent of two concentric outer ditches. These bulge outwards toward the King's
Stables, another Bronze Age monument. Although we can classify Haughey's Fort
in archaeological terminology as a 'hillfort', this in itself does not bring us much
closer to understanding its functions, be they social, economic, military or religious.

The 'King's Stables' has a specific name that testifies to a strong local folklore
tradition. It does not, however, tell us anything about the original function of the
monument. Nevertheless, it is worth observing that, if a monument was built in the
Neolithic period or in the Bronze Age (as was the King's Stables) and survived as a
site of veneration up to the Iron Age, the primary significance for *Iron Age* studies
is how it was perceived at that time and not what the original builders intended it to
be in the more remote past. Beliefs about the monument in the Iron Age may have
been very different from those of the original builders.

There is a cluster of what appear to be ploughed-down circular enclosures or
ring-ditches in flat pasture 300m north of the King's Stables. These were noted by
Barrie Hartwell on aerial photographs and may be of Bronze Age or Iron Age date.
There are also references to other destroyed sites in the area such as standing stones.
The Early Christian period is represented by the small enclosure known as the
'Abbey' in Ballybrolly townland, 1km north-east of Navan, and by a large circular
enclosure in Ballydoo townland, 300m west of Haughey's Fort.

A small investigation was carried out at the 'Abbey' in 1978. It is a low rocky
knoll enclosed by a slight earthwork. The interior was occupied by a two-chambered
structure delimited by thick drystone wall footings. A few finds suggested an Early

Christian date, so it is not impossible that the site was connected with one of the major ecclesiastical establishments in Armagh that documentary evidence suggests may have had lands in the area. There are several stretches of double-ditch earthworks running mainly north–south in Tray, Creeveroe and Tirearly townlands. They seem to divide the landscape between Haughey's Fort and Navan Fort. No site has been identified in the Navan area as a settlement of the Early Christian period, such as a rath or ringfort. This absence of settlement evidence for the Early Christian period is unusual in an area of this size.

Richard Warner suggested that the lack of settlement indicated the continuing ceremonial significance of the area. A related factor may be that the area was, as later sources indicate, church property from an early date, where the occupants were prevented from rath construction or did not build them because they were not needed or were not appropriate. But one feature probably dating from the Early Christian period, or even older, survives to the present day. This is the road referred to in early documents as *Botharemne* (Navan Road) that runs due west from Armagh, over the River Callan, and passes immediately to the south of Navan. This was replaced by the present road to Killylea only in the nineteenth century. Where the road ran over Leggar Hill, just west of the Callan, it skirted an early cemetery and a holy well to the south (see p. 88).

Stray finds

Many stray finds of archaeological material have been made over the last two centuries in the vicinity of Navan Fort. Some of these have been lost subsequently, but others are in museum collections. The oldest report, however, of a find from Navan is what appears to have been a broad-bladed bronze ceremonial weapon known as a 'halberd', probably dating from the Early Bronze Age. It was described in the medieval annals (*Chronicum Scotorum*) as having been found at Emain Macha in around AD 1115. The stray finds from the immediate vicinity of Navan can be grouped in order of antiquity. They begin with 'Bann Flakes' of the Mesolithic period and flint flakes and polished stone axes of the Neolithic period. Several flint artefacts, such as arrowheads and a 'discoidal knife', from 'Navan Rath' testify to activity in the Early Bronze Age. The Middle Bronze Age is represented by a bronze dagger found near the 'great Navan rath' in January 1852.

The Late Bronze Age, which began in around 1200 BC, is represented by several spearheads and socketed axes. The Early Iron Age is represented by a series of safety-pin brooches, or fibulae (Fig. 45), and other openwork brooches, termed 'Navan type', with pins held by a ball-and-socket arrangement. Other Iron Age objects discovered as stray finds include a decorated bronze mount, several bronze spear-butts and, most recently, the bronze terminal of a 'Y-shaped leading-piece'. The latter are characteristic Irish Iron Age bronze objects. They are sometimes found with horse-bits and are thought to have been used as part of a harness.

Early Christian penannular brooches

Four Early Christian period penannular brooches, dating from the sixth or seventh century AD, have been found in or near Navan Fort as stray finds (Fig. 46). This

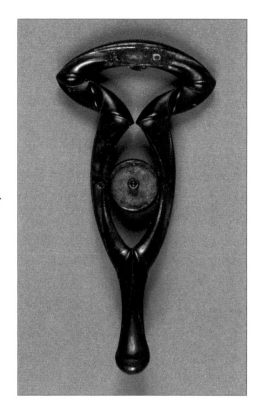

Fig. 45—Iron Age 'safety-pin' brooch found near Navan. The central setting probably contained enamel (photo: National Museum of Ireland).

group of rare finds is augmented by two others found in excavations, one from Navan Fort, Site A, and the other from an excavation on the site of the proposed visitor centre in the summer of 1991. The latter, the 'Ballyrea Brooch', was very fragmentary, but enough survived to show that it was made of cast bronze and its decorated terminals had cast interlaced knots, with a panel of amber on the reverse. This was a well-made ornament, decorated with gilding, amber and glass. It probably dates from the late ninth century AD. These prestige Early Christian period objects lack an obvious archaeological context in the area, that is, they do not appear to have been associated with a settlement site where someone important enough to wear one would have lived. This even applies to the two from excavations. The brooch from Site A was found at an intermediate level in the fill of the ditch of an older monument (a ring-barrow), while that from Ballyrea, though in the edge of a shallow gully, could not be said to have come from an occupation site of a well-defined type. The brooches are objects that would have been at home in a high-status rath or crannog, the dwelling-places of wealthy people. Here they apparently occur as objects accidentally lost. In so doing, they form an unusual concentration and testify to the intensive use of the landscape by people of some wealth and status long after Navan had been abandoned and Armagh had become the paramount religious centre.

Palynology: the study of ancient pollen
Most plants produce pollen, which blows around in the air and fertilises other plants

Fig. 46—Brooch found near Navan Fort, fifth century AD (photo: Ulster Museum).

of the same species. Pollen grains are coated in a very durable plastic-like material that does not rot in the same way as plant cellulose, for example. Pollen grains can survive for thousands of years in the ground, particularly in damp, peaty or muddy conditions. Every species of plant produces pollen grains of a distinct and identifiable form, with the result that the pollen of all of our commonest plants can readily be identified under a microscope. In a given sample of soil from which several hundred pollen grains have been extracted and identified in the laboratory, the numbers of pollen grains of different species present are counted. This provides an estimate of the proportions of the species growing around the sample point. But the picture is more complicated in that some plants produce more pollen than others and some pollens travel further in the wind than others. This results in a distortion of the proportions of the species, but, from studies of the behaviour of modern plants, palynologists can allow for these factors. This information has immense significance for archaeology because it enables scientists to work out the vegetational history of a place from a study of the 'pollen rain' over a long period.

The ideal circumstances for such a study are provided by a peat bog, which preserves everything that falls on it. The pollen is buried among the accumulating remains of bog plants, which do not rot completely. The bog grows upward gradually, thereby preserving the history of the changing species in the pollen record stretching back over thousands of years. Simply stated, a vertical core is extracted from the bog; the peat is sampled every few centimetres, starting at the bottom; and samples of the peat are radiocarbon dated. This complicated procedure, which is carried out in the School of Archaeology and Palaeoecology in Queen's University, gives the opportunity to study the vegetational history of a place from early prehistory to the present day. The layered mud from the beds of inter-drumlin lakes may contain a record of the history of the surrounding vegetation that is very useful to archaeologists, but the mud layers cannot be dated as easily as the peat from bogs.

Dave Weir of Queen's University has made a major contribution to the study of the Navan Complex from his work on pollen cores extracted from Loughnashade. He showed that in the early part of the Bronze Age, about 1900–1000 BC, there was a gradual increase in the percentage of grass pollen up to a maximum of 27 per cent. In the same period, an increase in the proportion of cereal-type pollens provided evidence for an increase in the extent of arable cultivation in the area of Navan. This corresponds with evidence from other sites, suggesting overall that this was a period with relatively warm, dry growing seasons.

In the early part of the Late Bronze Age (1200–600 BC) this phase of agricultural expansion seems to have come to an abrupt end, with a sudden decline in grasses and an increase in tree pollen. This also corresponds with evidence from other sites in Ireland and Europe and suggests that climate conditions changed from relative seasonality (hot summers, cool winters) to wetter, cooler conditions like those of today.

In the later part of the Late Bronze Age and the Early Iron Age (from about 600 BC to 100 BC) a gradual expansion of grassland and a contraction of woodland are indicated by the proportions of pollen types from Loughnashade. This suggests an increase of the use of the land for pasture because there is no evidence for an upsurge in the proportions of pollen from plants normally associated with cultivation, such as cereals. The pollen deposits in Loughnashade gave clear evidence for a period of marked woodland regeneration in the Iron Age (200 BC to AD 300). There was a sudden decrease in grasses and an increase in woodland pollen. Hazel and ash were the first to increase markedly, but elm also increased from less than 1 per cent to a maximum of 13 per cent. Grasses dropped to between 5 and 7 per cent, and pollen of other species indicating human disturbance (such as plantain) decreased to their lowest values since the early part of the Bronze Age. This phase of woodland regeneration can be traced at other sites in Ireland and is interpreted by Dave Weir as clear evidence for a reduction in population brought about by climatic deterioration. This is, of course, the period in which the mound was built on the Navan hilltop and other ceremonial activities took place in the area, such as the deposition of the bronze horns in Loughnashade. One wonders whether the apparent upsurge in monumental and religious activities was in part triggered by climate. This must simply remain an interesting question, as the vegetational, and by inference climatic, events recorded in Loughnashade cannot at present be dated so accurately that we can say whether the effects would have been noticeable in the 90s BC.

The end of the Iron Age and the beginning of the Early Christian period (from about AD 200 to 1000) is marked by a widespread clearance of the woodland and its replacement by a fully developed arable agricultural system that lasted, with some changes, to the present day. The cereal pollen levels recorded from Loughnashade at this time are among the highest from any site or period in Ireland and Britain. Dave Weir suggests that this may have to do with an influx to the area of new people, agricultural techniques and possibly cereal types more suited to the damper climate. The widespread adoption of the rotary quern for grinding grain at this time is an example of the improved technology in food preparation. There appears to be a temporary decrease in the volume of cereal during the sixth century, perhaps corresponding with a widespread but short-lived deterioration in climatic conditions during the AD 540s, detectable in narrow tree-rings and indicated in historical sources for the period.

The pollen work in and around Navan Fort is significant in that it brings the history of the landscape to life: it clothes it with a changing vegetation of trees, grasses and cultivated crops, with significant implications for interpreting the way of life of the people who lived there. It tells us about changing patterns of agriculture and climate, and it ties Navan into the larger story in Ireland and Britain of changing land-use, social organisation and climate. It also helps to put the archaeological evidence from excavated sites and the monuments themselves into an environmental context. Future research might seek to further reconcile evidence from the sites themselves with the local environmental picture. For example, can the evidence for Neolithic agriculture be related to the construction of monuments in the Navan landscape during the same period? The animal bones and cereal-processing from Haughey's Fort provide evidence for prosperous agriculture. Does this fit with the pollen evidence for changes in the early part of the Late Bronze Age? Was the construction of Navan Fort and its ceremonial mound triggered by circumstances related to those that brought about woodland regeneration at the expense of agriculture in the Iron Age?

Chapter 7

Navan in ancient tradition

The ancient topography of Navan Fort

So far we have discussed Navan Fort and its archaeology largely from an observational and scientific point of view. Before we can attempt to reach any rounded view of what the site might have meant or symbolised to people in the past, we must work out how the site and its associated features were portrayed in Early Christian sources. These sources are annalistic, genealogical, poetic and literary and provide evidence that may for present purposes be interpreted in historical, literary or mythological contexts. Attempts to assess what was the significance of the site and the monuments to those who built them are highly speculative. We have no inscriptions or images, and the later literary material can with safety be taken to refer only to the period in which it was written. We will return to these issues again, but in the meantime I will briefly review the Early Christian and medieval lore and, by implication, the interpretation of the site in those periods. This task has been simplified by extensive articles by Jim Mallory and others in the report on the 1960s excavations in Navan Fort and in various issues of *Emania*.

History and proto-history

The monument we know today as Navan Fort was known in the past as Emain or Emain Macha (another important place, Aenach Macha, was also situated somewhere in the area). In early place-name lore other sites were described in relation to Emain (Macha), showing that everyone knew where it was. According to the Annals of the Four Masters, compiled in around AD 1600 from older materials, Emain Macha entered 'history' in 'the year of the world' (*anno mundi*) 3579 (that is, around 1621 BC): 'Conmael, son of Emer, having been thirty years in the sovereignty of Ireland, fell, in the battle of Aenach Macha...'. In a year that approximately equates with 654 BC, the same annals inform us that 'Macha

81

Mongruadh...was slain by Reachtaidh Righdhearg...It was Macha that commanded the sons of Dithorba (after bringing them into servitude) to erect the fort of Eamhain, that it might be the chief city of Ulster for ever'. In the entry for a year corresponding to around 542 BC the Annals of Clonmacnoise record the foundation of the City of Rome, but, perhaps to establish precedence, add that 'Finn McBaicke reigned then in Eawinn [Emain] Macha as King of Ulster'!

In the first century BC the annals record the names of nine kings who, it is claimed, ruled in Emain for various periods, beginning with Enda mac Rochada in about 96 BC. The annals date the birth of CuChulainn (the champion of Ulster) to 34 BC. The 60-year reign of Conchobar mac Nessa, the most famous legendary king of Ulster based at Emain Macha, began in 30 BC or 20 BC, and the Cattle Raid of Cooley took place in 19 BC. In the first three centuries AD the annals record the names of fourteen kings of Emain, but the succession came to an end in around AD 331 when, according to the Annals of the Four Masters, the battle of Achadh-leithdheirg in Farney (a part of County Monaghan) was fought by the three Collas against the Ulstermen, 'in which fell Fearghus Fogha...the last king of Ulster, [who resided] at Eamhain. They afterwards burned Eamhain, and the Ulstermen did not dwell therein since. They also took from the Ulstermen that part of the province [extending] from the Righe [Newry River] and Loch n-Eathach [Lough Neagh] westwards.'

This is the pivotal reference for much of what has since been written and speculated about the early history of Ulster. Although the date and details may be disputed, many authorities believe that this account of the fall of Emain contributes to an explanation of the political reality of Ulster when history 'proper' begins in the late sixth century AD. At that time the area around Emain, including Armagh, Fermanagh and Monaghan, was occupied by the Airgialla ('hostage-givers'), a subject tribe of the Uí Néill. The Ulaidh territory was confined to Antrim and Down, yet the consistent and unchallenged tradition looked back to a time when 'the Ulstermen' ruled from Emain over the whole of the ancient 'fifth', or province, of Ulster.

Subsequent references to Emain Macha in the Irish annals include: in AD 759 there was a battle between the Uí Néill and the Ulaidh at Emain; in 1005 Brian Boru camped in Emain while visiting Armagh; in 1103 another O'Brian, this time Muircheartach, did the rounds of Aenach-Macha (the 'assembly-place' of Emain), Emain and Armagh (where he left 8 ounces of gold on the altar); and in 1145 we have seen that a lime-kiln was built by Gillamacliag, successor of St Patrick (archbishop of Armagh) opposite Emain. Finally, it is recorded that in 1387 a house was built in Emain by Niall Ua Neill, for the entertainment of the learned men of Ireland, 'for there was not any house within it for a long time till then'. These references are few because Emain was deserted and unoccupied throughout the early historic period, but they are significant because almost all record royal visits or activities. The battle of 759 may have been a turning point in an attempt by the Ulaidh to recover their lost territory, choosing as the battleground the legendary headquarters of their ancient patrimony. Both of the kings of Munster, Brian Boru and Muircheartach, were also kings of all Ireland at the times of their visits to

Emain, a place consistently associated with ancient kingship. No doubt this connection was one of the reasons for recording the visits in the first place. The account of the construction of the lime-kiln can be seen merely as a record of something marvellous: it was 'sixty feet every way'. But it also reminds us that Emain lay in an area that appears to have been granted to the church in Armagh by Daire Derg from before the dawn of history, according to tradition. This takeover of the old sites by the new religion is emphasised in early sources, and a similar emphasis may lie behind the reference to the archbishop's lime-kiln at Emain. While it may not have been considered appropriate to build a church in Navan, the abbot had no misgivings about using the stone as well as the lime from Emain, presumably for a major building project in Armagh itself.

The reference to the building of a house in Emain for the learned men by O'Neill is intriguing from several aspects, chiefly because its site is unknown so far. Other, contemporaneous literary sources, such as the Registers of the Archbishops of Armagh, testify to ongoing disputes between the O'Neills and the church over the land around Emain while the O'Neills were attempting to expand their patrimony. The building of the hostel in Emain for learned men may have been a symbolic part of the ongoing campaign, perhaps harking back to the ancient hostels on the site associated with the legends of King Conchobar. Not even an archbishop would have been immune from satire if he attempted to deny learned men the hospitality provided by an influential magnate.

Navan Fort/Emain in the literature

There is some debate about whether Emain Macha, the site identified as Navan Fort (from an anglicisation of *An Eamhain*), was one of the places in Ireland listed with coordinates in Ptolemy of Alexandria's gazetteer of the known world, dating from the second century AD. The place in question was called *Isamnion* by Ptolemy, and some linguists have claimed that this may be derived from a word like *Emain*. Several possible English meanings have been ascribed to the first element of the place-name Emain Macha; for example, it could mean 'neck-brooch', referring to that which the founding goddess, Macha, was believed to have used to mark out the enclosure. The use of the brooch 'explained' why the enclosure appears to be awry on the hill. It was because Macha could reach further in front than behind with the brooch. Or Emain could mean 'twin', alluding to the twins borne by the goddess Macha in one of the foundation legends of the site. The second element of the name, Macha, is normally taken to refer to the goddess of the locality. As we have seen, she is involved in foundation legends of the site and is associated with names and legends of the Ulster kingship. It has been suggested that Macha originally meant 'a plain or pasture' and may have been a local place-name, eventually elevated into the concept of a goddess. The literary and mythological personage Macha is comparable, however, with a number of other sovereignty goddesses of Ireland, such as Medb and Tailtiu. I will return to this theme below but for the moment must emphasise the potential significance of the place-name of the site now known as Navan Fort, associating it with a goddess queen and possibly twins or a neck-brooch.

The fame of Emain stems from its portrayal in Early Irish literature as the capital of the Ulaidh in the 'Ulster Cycle' of tales. About 80 of the tales have survived, and they were written between the seventh and the fourteenth century, although no manuscripts survive from before the eleventh century. Do the tales include very ancient traditions transmitted by word of mouth for generations before they were written down? Or were they initially composed as written texts and, therefore, contain material relevant only to the time when they were written? The view of the past portrayed in the tales would be those of the writers of the time. There is no doubt that the tales deliberately set themselves in the past, generally in the first century BC, and portray a political and intellectual landscape that was in many ways unlike the situation in the Early Christian and early medieval periods when they were written down.

The tales depict a heroic society in which the Ulstermen were usually portrayed sympathetically as justified, warlike defenders of their land. Emain was depicted as a royal headquarters where the king, Conchobar, had his court with his advisor, Cathbad, the druid, and his champions CuChulainn and Conall Cernach. It resembles the Troy of the Homeric poems or the Camelot of the Arthurian legends. The most impressive, longest and most influential of the tales is the *Táin bó Cuailgne*, the 'Cattle Raid of Cooley'. This story describes how Queen Medb of Connacht led the forces of Ireland against the Ulstermen in order to capture the prized bull of Cooley. The Ulster heroes muster at Emain and set off to the south-west to intercept the Connacht army. The story is full of diversions and sub-plots but ends with the defeat of the Connacht army and a fight in which the brown bull of Cooley destroys Medb's bull. In the process it gave names to a number of places along the route of the fight. Jim Mallory has surveyed the descriptions of Emain in the tales and has identified a number of features of the site that survive to the present day and appear to be referred to in the tales.

Emain is often referred to as a fortified site, a *dún*, or 'fort', and its interior is called a *les* or *liss*. These are terms used from the seventh century to describe the layout of a defended settlement of the time, now known as a rath or ringfort. This suggests that Emain was envisaged or deliberately portrayed as a large and prestigious secular settlement. The surrounding rampart was described as a *dóu*, where personages in the tales often sat. The main mound, Site B, seems to be referred to as *Duma na nGiall i nEmain*, 'the mound of the hostages in Emain', in *Táin bó Cuailnge* and as the *sídbruig*, or 'fairy mound', of Emain in other sources. The tales sometimes refer to buildings in Emain; for example, according to a twelfth-century source:

Conchobor had three houses, the *Croebhruad* (ruddy-branch), and the *Teite Brecc* and the *Crobderg* (red-branch). In the *Crobderg* were the heads and the spoils. In the *Croebruadh* were the kings...In the *Teite Brecc*, there were the spears and the shields and the swords.

The townland immediately west of Navan is Creeveroe (*Craobhruadh*). It has been suggested that the original *Croebruadh* was the inauguration tree of the Ulster dynasty, but it is usually depicted as the main royal palace of Conchobar and his warriors. In one eleventh-century source it is described as follows:

> Nine compartments were in it from the fire to the wall. Thirty feet was the height of each bronze partition in the house, carvings of red yew therein. A wooden floor beneath, and a roofing of tiles above...The twelve cubicles of the twelve chariot-chiefs were round about the king's compartment. Games and music and singing there, heroes performing their feats, poets singing, harpers and players on the tympans striking up their sounds.

This description is rather formulaic and is applied in the tales to heroic halls at other places. It seems to be a fanciful expansion and elaboration of a large round house of the Early Christian period with a central fireplace. The outlines of many examples of such round houses have been found in excavations of raths and ringforts dating from the seventh to the ninth century AD. Slightly more archaic descriptions of other royal palaces describe 'Seven ranks there (and) and seven compartments (from fire to wall)...Three posts of bronze in the (?) of the house. House of oak with roof of shingles.' This reminds us that the first century BC multi-ring timber structure excavated in Navan was made entirely of oak; there were seven spaces between the central post and the outer wall; and there were three parallel aisles (p. 29). One question immediately arises: could the large wooden building on the Navan hilltop have been the inspiration for the description in the tales of a large circular wooden building in Emain? Is the tradition of a building in the tales a genuine inheritance of a past reality? The answer is, probably, no. Navan and the other sites with large buildings described in the literature, such as Bricriu's house, were perceived in the Early Christian and medieval periods as high-status residences, as royal strongholds with palaces and all the necessary trappings of a warrior aristocracy. In this light the descriptions of the palaces in the tales can be interpreted as fanciful expansions of contemporary dwellings where everything is larger and made of rare, costly materials. While the possibility that the tales contain a historical memory of something that actually happened seems unlikely, we will meet an even more intriguing possibility later.

Chapter 8

Recent developments

The story of research in and around Navan/Emain Macha continues to the present, so that the material in this book represents only a summary of the state of archaeological knowledge about the site in 2003. When set up in 1986 the Navan Research Group developed a research strategy for Navan Fort and the other sites, known and unknown, within the general area of the Navan Complex. At that time, further excavation in Navan itself was ruled out because the report on the earlier excavations had not been published. The research strategy involved the identification of sites in the area using aerial photography and geophysical survey techniques, to be followed up by small-scale excavations to determine the age and nature of the features examined. The series of excavations in Haughey's Fort was also a major component of the programme. Naturally, in the absence of personnel dedicated to the programme, its implementation depended on individuals with the necessary expertise being able to make time among other responsibilities, on the availability of finance and on permission from landowners to survey and excavate on their land.

Jim Mallory was able to dedicate some of his summer research time to the Haughey's Fort project and in the process drew in valuable contributions from Queen's University-based environmentalists and research students. This work was centred on Haughey's Fort, and the various studies associated with it have revolutionised our understanding of the development of the site itself and the surrounding landscape. Little was happening in terms of archaeological investigation elsewhere in the Navan area at the time, as the writer was preoccupied, as time permitted, with publishing the report on the 1960s excavations. Notable exceptions are the aerial photographic surveys published in 1987 and 1991 by Barrie Hartwell and the studies of sites and stray finds published by Richard Warner in 1984 and 1986. The evidence from Navan, the Dorsey and Haughey's Fort for the dating of the sites, using dendrochronology and radiocarbon analysis, stimulated a series of papers from Mike Baillie. He discussed ways of refining the dating of parts of the complex and the wider environmental issues raised by the existence of the sites, the dating evidence for them and contemporaneous developments elsewhere.

Legarhill

In 1989 the Historic Monuments Branch was informed of bulldozing for a new recreation area on the top of Legarhill (formerly Mullaghcreevie), one of the drumlins between Navan and Armagh. The River Callan flows immediately to the east, where it is crossed by a picturesque old stone bridge. This is the successor of a medieval wooden bridge over which ran Botharemne, the old road west from Armagh. The road ran over Legarhill and continued past the southern side of Navan Fort. A picture map of Armagh made in 1601 by Richard Bartlett (Fig. 47) shows a ruined church on the top of the hill, and it was hoped that surveillance of the bulldozing would reveal traces of its foundations and provide a focus for formal excavation. Traces of two sets of foundations, one of which may be post-medieval, were found. The line of the ancient roadway was identified as a sunken hollow-way some 2m wide and 50cm deep, running down the eastern side of the hill toward

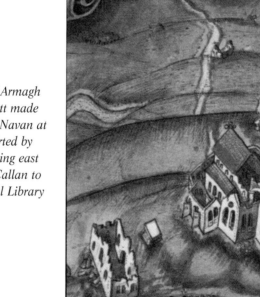

Fig. 47—Map of Armagh by Richard Bartlett made in 1601 showing Navan at the top (west) skirted by the old road running east across the River Callan to Armagh (National Library of Ireland).

Callan Bridge. The ancient road ran some 20m to the north of the present lane over Legarhill and on the lower slopes of the hill formed the northern limit of a cemetery of shallow graves, probably of medieval date. The burials were most numerous north of St Patrick's Well, venerated when the water was said to rise in it on the eve of the feast of SS Peter and Paul (29 June), patrons of the Abbey of Armagh. The well, a natural hollow in the limestone, was shaded by an old thorn tree to which rags and other offerings were tied as votive tokens. The well and tree have recently been sundered from their landscape setting and historical context. They now stand incongruously in a modern housing estate.

The Navan Centre

As a result of the debate over the significance of Navan raised by the Friends of Navan in the public inquiry in 1985 and by the decision to prevent further quarrying in the area, the Navan Fort Initiative Group was set up by government in the late 1980s. Its remit was to explore ways of bringing better information about the site to the public and tourists, with the knowledge that considerable funds were available for development. Not surprisingly, the group recommended that a visitor centre to interpret Navan for the public, tourists and schools should be built at the site. After some debate, a site for the centre was chosen some 350m south-west of Navan Fort (Fig. 48). The main funding for the building of the centre and its fitting out was donated by the International Fund for Ireland, and the building of the centre and its subsequent management were entrusted to the charitable trust Navan at Armagh, set up in 1989. The centre was opened in June 1993 and contains archaeological and

Fig. 48—Aerial view of Navan Centre from the west; carpark right, buildings centre left (photo: Mick Aston).

mythological displays on the Navan landscape, an educational section and the usual visitor facilities. One of the aims of the Navan at Armagh Trust is to protect the landscape of Navan Fort, and to this end the trust bought some areas of land using grants from the National Heritage Memorial Fund. These include fields near Navan Fort in Ballyrea and Creeveroe, parts of Haughey's Fort and the margins of Loughnashade. Unfortunately the number of people visiting the centre has not matched expectations, and the facility closed in June 2001, but at the time of writing it is hoped that the centre will reopen and continue the good work it espoused, particularly in education, providing information and landscape protection.

In preparation for specifying archaeological works necessary before construction of the centre, several trial-pits were excavated across the proposed site in the spring of 1991. These revealed little of archaeological interest, and the entire area of the proposed visitor centre was mechanically cleared of topsoil under the supervision of a team of archaeologists from Queen's University, Belfast, employed by Navan at Armagh. Subsequent hand-excavation of the 40m-by-80m site revealed few features of potential archaeological interest—some pits and hollows and drainage trenches of indeterminate age. Finds, however, were more interesting, including a significant collection of flint flakes, a piece of a 'plano-convex knife', and a flint axe. The flint objects and a few small sherds of pottery testify to some occupation on the visitor centre site during the Neolithic period, *c.* 4000–2500 BC. The decorated bronze brooch of the ninth century AD described earlier was found in the edge of a shallow gully in the carpark area. It testifies to the (not unexpected) presence of people of some status in the area at that time but on its own tells nothing of the nature and location of their settlement.

In 1992 the 'footprint' of the centre had to be extended to the west in an area some 10m by 20m. This was excavated by Norman Crothers, who found a sizeable ditch traversing the area from north-west to south-east over a distance of 16m. A ^{14}C date from the ditch centring on *c.* AD 750 accorded with the date of the pieces of Early Christian pottery ('souterrain ware') found in the field. Possibly the feature delimited a settlement or a field system. The skeleton of a juvenile was found in a shallow grave dug through the upper fill of the ditch. A ^{14}C date indicated that the young person had died between about AD 1500 and AD 1650. The burial was sealed by a layer containing pieces of a kind of coarse, late medieval pottery typical of east Ulster, called 'everted-rim ware'. This relatively random examination of a small piece of the landscape around Navan Fort shows the wealth of information of all periods that still lies there and that requires protection and, ultimately, research.

Geophysics

In 1993 a group of archaeologists from the US visited Northern Ireland and included Navan Fort on a short study tour, a spin-off of a larger get-together in Britain sponsored by the British Council. One of them was Professor Dan Larson of California State University, who at that time was pioneering the use of geophysical survey techniques in the US. Larson was invited by the Navan Research Group to return to Navan in the following year to carry out geophysical surveys to locate buried archaeological features in the 'Fort' in addition to the two known upstanding monuments, Sites A and B. The techniques deployed by the US team included ground-penetrating radar and magnetometry (Fig. 49). With the former, radar signals are reflected from contrasting deposits in the ground, giving different patterns on a read-out or screen depending on the nature of the material and its depth. Magnetometry works by measuring the earth's magnetic field at close-set intervals and mapping variations visually. Where the soil has been disturbed, for whatever reason, the strength of the earth's magnetic field is altered locally. Thus archaeological features can sometimes be detected and their outlines plotted on a plan. These geophysics techniques do not always work because different subsoils and the underlying rock type can mask the slighter variations caused by archaeological features.

An area to the east of the main mound, Site B, in Navan Fort was gridded out for survey in the hope of finding palisade trenches running across the hilltop, the extensions of those found by Waterman in his excavations under the mound at the entrances to the northern circles of the Iron Age figures of eight. We did not find the palisade slots where expected. Instead, the geophysicists identified a circular feature some 30m in diameter immediately north-west of Site A (Fig. 50). The ring was defined by two concentric anomalies about 2m apart, probably representing narrow infilled ditches or foundation slots for wooden walls. This feature was so well defined that it could be concluded that the magnetic anomaly producing its outline was probably generated by burnt material in its fill. Given the size of the double circle, it was immediately assumed to be of Iron Age date by comparison with the

Fig. 49—Dan Larson and Beth Ambos of California State University demonstrating ground-penetrating radar to Stephen Gilmore in Navan Fort in 1994 (photo: J. Finegan).

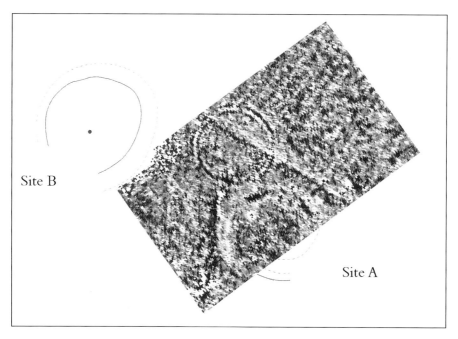

Fig. 50—Results of the first geophysical survey at Navan. The 'new ring', Site C, appears as the top of a figure of eight, the base of which is formed by the ring found under Site A in 1961.

other large rings already excavated at the site. Furthermore, its position in relation to Site A suggested that it might be the larger, northern element of a figure-of-eight structure like those of Phase 3 (i–ii) found nearby under the mound at Site B. The southern element would have been the set of triple wall-slots found by Dudley Waterman in Site A, Phase A, in 1961 (see p. 12). Testing of this exciting new discovery by excavation had to await publication of the report on the 1960s excavations and took place between 1999 and 2002 (p. 98).

The *Time Team*

Early in 1996 Tim Taylor, the producer of an archaeological television series, approached the Department of the Environment to see if he could make a programme about the King's Stables. The series was called *Time Team*, and the pattern was that a 'local person' or antiquarian informed the team about an intriguing archaeological puzzle that they hoped to 'solve', or at least seriously address, over a weekend of three days using the Time Team's expertise. The Time Team comprised four archaeologists with attendant specialists, including geophysicists, excavation supervisors, landscape surveyors and graphic artists. The presenter of the programme, Tony Robinson, acts as the 'layman' on site. He asks the archaeologists to explain what they are doing and gives occasional summaries. Only material filmed during the three days of the fieldwork is used in the programme. There can be no second thoughts, no going back and no supplementary material. For the viewer interested in archaeology, the format is exciting: you see everything as it happens; there are debates on site about the best way to proceed; and the discoveries are often fascinating. Some archaeologists have misgivings about trying to do too much in three days and sacrificing science for the sake of a television programme. The team are themselves aware of the issues, which are generally addressed by careful advance planning (they only work where they are likely to find something of interest) and by post-excavation research and analysis, unfortunately not covered in the programmes. Before expressing an interest in the Navan area, the programme-makers had already transmitted two successful series and attracted a UK audience of several millions.

Tim Taylor had seen an article in the periodical *Current Archaeology* in which I referred to Navan as an Iron Age sanctuary and to the King's Stables as perhaps a place of sacrifice. He hoped that a *Time Team* programme could examine the concept of sacrifice in a prehistoric context by excavating some more of the King's Stables and by probing the margins of Loughnashade. After discussion, it was agreed that a programme, for the sake of the viewing audience, could be based on the proposition that one of the Ulster tales speaks of King Conchobar's 'three palaces'. It could be argued that we know of two of them—Navan Fort and Haughey's Fort—where then might the third lie? This was agreed as the scenario for the Navan-centred programme, but the sites to be excavated were chosen (with one exception) from the research agenda of the Navan Research Group. The programme was assisted by the Department of the Environment, which recruited a team of archaeologists under the direction of Mal Conway to carry out the excavation. The aim was to make sure that the fieldwork would be controlled, run, licensed and carried out by a locally based and funded team, onto which the Time Team was superimposed for the sake of the programme.

Filming started on a Friday at the end of April with the opening of a trench across the double-ditched cropmarks shown by aerial photographs of Creeveroe, about halfway between Navan and Haughey's Fort. At the same time a geophysical survey was carried out on the top of Creeveroe Hill and to the south in the townland of Ballyrea (said to translate into English as 'place of the kings'). Both of these drew a blank. Conchobar's 'third palace', or a plausible substitute, was not going to be that easy to find. As the person responsible for facilitating the Time Team operation at Navan and appearing in the programme as the 'local archaeologist' enlisting the team's assistance, I naturally had serious doubts about the whole operation. Would it go smoothly? Would there be good rapport with the landowners? Would all the people we depended on play their parts? Would our excavation techniques stand up to close inspection? And, most of all, would we find enough in three days to make an interesting programme for the viewing public, showing the area in a good light?

An early setback was that we could not get access to one of the three sites targeted for definite excavation, but there was no need for concern. The excavations were otherwise exemplary. The sun shone warmly. And in fact we found far more than I would have dared to 'plant' in the hope of making a good programme. We had been stripping topsoil for only a few minutes at the Creeveroe site when part of a Neolithic ground stone axe was discovered. The excitement of the Time Team's archaeologist was palpable as he described it by radio (on camera) to his colleagues at the 'incident room' in the Navan Centre. From then on, things got hectic, and the following three days were a memorable rush of discoveries. The Time Team kept three camera crews in the field continuously, which, with their back-up staff of specialists, researchers and production assistants, amounted to 30 people. Everyone kept in touch with what was happening at the various sites by radio.

The Creeveroe excavation soon began to reveal the upper edges of the two parallel ditches shown in the aerial photographs. One began to produce large quantities of bun-shaped lumps of slag ('furnace bottoms'), left by early iron-smelting processes, from its upper fill. The fill of the western ditch was cleaner, but near the bottom was a layer of charcoaly soil with a few animal bones, evidently deposited not long after the feature was made. Most significantly, the bones were accompanied by some sherds of what was unmistakably Late Bronze Age pottery. This was an incredible stroke of luck because linear ditches are very difficult to date by trying to find artefacts in small sample excavations. Remember that the double-ditched feature is over 1km long, and yet a 2m-wide section yielded good dating evidence in a little over one day's digging! If only it were always so easy! The conclusion was that the double-ditched feature was made in the Bronze Age and was possibly associated with the Bronze Age activity at Haughey's Fort to the west. The excavated section of eastern trench had been reused as a dump nearly 3000 years later in the Early Christian period. If there had not been Bronze Age material in the western ditch, we would probably have concluded mistakenly that the ditches were cut in the Early Christian period, sometime between AD 600 and AD 1000. This would have distorted other interpretations, mainly appreciation of the extent of the monumental development of the landscape in the Bronze Age.

While this was going on, work had started on a section of the line of the middle rampart of Haughey's Fort. Earlier in the day, geophysics had shown that the ditch bulged out toward the King's Stables and there appeared to be a gap in it, possibly an entrance causeway, aligned on a similar gap in the outer rampart also in the direction of King's Stables. A trench was opened over one side of the gap by Dermot Moore and his team. They did indeed uncover what appeared to be the southern side of a gateway, marked by a large post-pit. There was a gap in the ditch, and across it ran a cobbled pathway at right angles. The path ran out of the trench downslope toward the gap in the outer rampart shown by geophysics. The southern side of the path was flanked by a row of smaller post- and stake-holes, probably for a fence (Fig. 51). The excavation trench was not wide enough (it had to be kept small owing to the time constraints) to reveal the northern side of the gateway and road, but presumably that side was also fenced to control access between the entrance road and the space between the outer two ramparts. Sherds of Bronze Age pottery and parts of two rubbing-stones used to grind grain by hand (saddle querns) were found in the entrance gap. Again, this little excavation was extraordinarily successful. Two days' work demonstrated the existence of the entrance gap in the middle ditch, located one side of a gate and exposed a fenced cobbled track running downhill toward the outer rampart and the King's Stables. Like the excavations on the Creeveroe ditches, all this was completely new and dramatic testimony to the nature

Fig. 51—Filming at the entrance to Haughey's Fort. The Time Team *producer, Tim Taylor, points to the features to be recorded while the 'team' waits to begin discussion.*

of the Bronze Age infrastructure around Haughey's Fort.

Stuart Ainsworth, a specialist in landscape archaeology with the Time Team, noticed a field boundary on his map making an intriguing semicircle on plan in Ballydoo townland, about 1km west of Navan. He surmised that this might be a remnant of a large earthwork enclosure and, since it was in line with Navan and Haughey's Fort and of considerable size, that it could be used in the programme as a contender for Conchobar's 'third palace'. This site was known to the Navan Research Group, and details were lodged in the Northern Ireland Sites and Monuments Record. It was believed to be an 'early ecclesiastical enclosure', a type of large, often circular earthwork of the Early Christian period in Ireland delimiting the sanctuary of an early church or monastic site. Only a few of these have been excavated, and remains of early churches (from before AD 900) are very scarce. Clearly, historical associations, place-names, early burial-markers, fragments of cross-carved stones and bullauns (hollowed-out boulders like crude fonts) can distinguish these as ecclesiastical sites from their generally smaller relatives, the secular raths or ringforts of contemporaneous landholders. Some early ecclesiastical earthwork enclosures were never abandoned and have been used for ecclesiastical purposes to the present day. The possible example in Ballydoo, however, had none of these attributes. It was believed to be an ecclesiastical enclosure mainly on account of its size and shape and because the next townland, Tamlaght Bo, was associated with a documented early church, site unknown.

The Time Team believed that it might be Iron Age and were keen to investigate. It seemed that even if it did turn out to be Early Christian period—later than the abandonment of Navan—it would still be useful to have some information about it, information that we might otherwise have taken years to glean. Thus, halfway through the three-day investigation, attention was suddenly focused on an entirely new site not in the original plan. The landowner readily gave his permission for the work to take place, and the geophysics team descended on the field. Their survey quickly showed that the semicircle had originally been a full circle making a bank-and-ditch enclosure some 100m in diameter and that there were several interesting areas of geophysical anomaly within it. After discussion Mal Conway laid out a long trench across the perimeter of the ploughed-down enclosure at what seemed to be an interesting spot and transferred his team from Creeveroe when work there came to an end on the Saturday afternoon.

The excavation in Ballydoo quickly revealed features and finds of the Early Christian and medieval periods. A fine medieval iron spur turned up on the first evening. The next day the excavations penetrated deep into the ditch, and some Early Christian period pottery was discovered. On the basis of this evidence the Time Team agreed that the enclosure was probably Early Christian, too late to have been an original 'third palace' but perhaps, they suggested, woven into the legend at a later date when Navan Fort, Haughey's Fort and Ballydoo were all extant and lying equally spaced as a line of prominent large enclosures in the landscape. The excavation carried on for two weeks after filming for the programme finished and revealed that the ditch of the Ballydoo enclosure had been recut sometime in the past. The Early Christian material was in the later section, so the original Ballydoo site could indeed be earlier. Other very interesting finds were crucibles, perhaps for metalworking, and a number of tiny rods of coloured glass twisted around one another. These were used in the Early Christian period for the manufacture of glass beads and other inlaid objects. They testify to the high status of the occupants of the Ballydoo enclosure. Although the manufacture of similar glass objects was carried out at ecclesiastical sites in Armagh at around the same time, there was no direct evidence for ecclesiastical use of the Ballydoo enclosure. At least we now know that it was used and probably built at the appropriate time for an early ecclesiastical site.

The *Time Team* weekend was a breathtaking experience for all involved. The work was driven by the need to make a coherent and interesting television programme, by the number of experts in various fields devoted for the three days to the problem and by the pressure to get good material for the viewers. Fortunately, everything went well: the sun shone; the area looked attractive; and the archaeological discoveries were unexpectedly prolific and useful. The research agenda of the Navan Research Group was pursued. We demonstrated the antiquity of the Creeveroe ditches; we proved that the Ballydoo site was indeed a large enclosure dating from the Early Christian period; and we located an entrance to Haughey's Fort overlooking the King's Stables. The often-repeated programme has also contributed to raising awareness far and wide of the archaeological interest of the area.

The date of Navan Fort

Until 1998 the comparison between the Dorsey and Navan Fort depended essentially on the identity in date of timber structures associated with the monuments. The date of construction of the earthwork enclosure, Navan Fort itself, was unknown, and there had been suggestions that it was older than the Iron Age, based on the analogy with the similar-looking Late Neolithic 'henge' monuments of southern Britain. With the publication in 1997 of the report on Waterman's excavations and the consequent lifting by the Department of the Environment of the moratorium on excavations, the way became clear to carry out further excavations at Navan Fort. Clearly, the first issue to address was the date of the monument itself. In 1998 Jim Mallory was commissioned to excavate a section across a damp area of the ditch of Navan Fort in the hope of recovering datable material (Fig. 52). The exercise was unexpectedly successful. Near the bottom of the ditch the crushed remains of an elegant lathe-turned wooden bowl were found. Parts of a large, squared and charred oak beam were also found lying on the ditch bottom (Fig. 53). It must have been placed there immediately after the ditch was dug. Tree-ring dating of the timber in Queen's University showed that it had been felled in the 90s BC, the same date as the timbers in the Navan mound and the timbers of the Dorsey palisade 17km to the south.

In so far as archaeology can demonstrate, Navan Fort and the Dorsey were built at the same time. At Navan a squared structural post provided the date for the ditch bottom. In the northern section of the Dorsey rough oak stumps were placed more haphazardly in the ditch. There may, however, be some shared concept between the actions at the two sites. We can only speculate that the burnt timber in the bottom of the Navan ditch may have been part of the charred remains of the multi-ring timber structure, the lower parts of which were buried in the mound (Phase 4, p. 28).

Fig. 52—Jim Mallory's 1998 excavation in the ditch of Navan Fort. The infill of soft peaty silt meant that the deep cut had to be stepped for safety (photo: Queen's University, Belfast).

Fig. 53—Carved oak beam lying in the bottom of the ditch of Navan Fort. The trowel on the right provides a scale (photo: Queen's University, Belfast).

Site C

We saw how in 1994 the geophysicists located a large circular anomaly, evidently an archaeological feature, some 30m in diameter immediately north-west of the ring-barrow, Site A. The position of the feature was identified on the ground surface by Dan Larson using an instrument known as a gradiometer for measuring small localised changes in the earth's magnetic field, so that the excavation trenches could be laid out directly over it. In 1999–2002 I took a small team to excavate several small trenches across parts of the perimeter of this double ring, now designated as 'Site C'. We wanted to discover its age and purpose. As soon as the topsoil was removed, the top of the fill of the feature was revealed where it was cut into the contrasting undisturbed subsoil. The strong outline on the geophysics plot had been created by burnt material—charcoal and reddened earth—in the upper fill of two concentric slots. There was, however, a third slot with a clean clay fill running between the other two. Thus the circular feature or structure was made up of three concentric slots, like those found nearby under the Site B mound in the 1960s excavations. The inner slot produced evidence that it had contained spaced vertical posts linked by a thinner vertical seam, usually interpreted as 'post-and-plank' walling. The middle slot, which appears to have been the first dug, lacked any evidence for structural remains or other deliberate features. Perhaps it was used at an initial stage in the setting out or construction of the feature.

The outermost slot was more V-shaped in profile, and burnt material (a mixture of red-burnt soil, charcoal and specks of cindery material indicating intense burning) ran down its inner slope and was covered by the cleaner main fill of the feature. There was some evidence that the burnt deposit resulted from the burning of wood emplaced in the slot, although some of the material could have slumped in later. The destruction by fire of the structure that stood in the inner slot was the same event that produced the layer of burning running down the outer edge of the outer slot. We have yet to arrive at a comprehensive explanation for the structural evidence presented by the concentric sets of slots.

An unusual feature was the volume of burnt bone found at intervals in the burnt deposits of the inner and outer slots. Over 2000 small pieces have been recovered, and Eileen Murphy has identified 58 to species. All are from animals and represent, in order of quantity, pig, cattle and sheep/goat, approximately reflecting the proportion of the three principal species of animal bone, presumed to be food refuse, in the, again presumed, 'occupation layer' of the Iron Age found under the Site B mound. There seems to be too much burnt bone in these deposits for it to have got there accidentally, and we have to consider seriously that it may represent the remains of a ceremony involving the cremation of animal remains.

Most exciting of all is the fact that, in examining the area where the triple ring found by D.M. Waterman in 1961 and Site C overlap, we have managed to determine that the slots of both rings join one another, outer to outer, middle to middle, and so on. In other words, Site C and Site A, Phase A, are one and the same feature, a giant figure-of-eight structure some 50m long! This is very similar to the figure-of-eight rings of Phase 3 (ii) found under the mound, but the latter were believed to be houses with larger attached yards on the north, and it was impossible to link the northern and southern elements with one another at the point of intersection. Site C, however, gives no indication that there was any functional difference between the northern and southern elements.

No finds of note have so far come from the Site C slots, but we were able to date them using radiocarbon analysis of the charcoal in their fill. Also, they cut through, and therefore were later than, one of the palisade slots found under the mound in the 1960s and dating from roughly 150 BC. The radiocarbon dates suggest that Site C is likely to date from before the beginning of the first century AD. So we have interpreted them as roughly contemporaneous with the construction of the fort and mound, but whether they date from a little before or after the mound we cannot at present suggest. These features are very puzzling and unusual, and it must be admitted that there is not as yet any convincing explanation of their constructional sequence, the wooden structure they contained or what ceremonial activity they might represent.

The latest season of excavation on Site C, in 2001, examined a short section on the eastern side of the larger, northern ring to look for an east-facing entrance. The figure-of-eight structures found under the Navan mound in the 1960s (Phase 3 (ii)) and the closely comparable 'Rose' phase at Knockaulin suggested that there should be an entrance gap here, flanked by palisade trenches running downhill to the east. This is exactly what was found at Site C. We found the northern side of a gap flanked by the beginning of a palisade slot running at right angles to the east (Fig. 54). If the analogy with Knockaulin holds good, it is likely that the east-facing entrance to Site C and its attendant palisade(s) point to the original entrance to

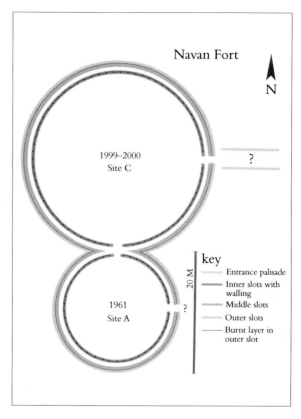

Fig. 54—Schematic representation of the relationship on plan of the triple ring-slot, figure-of-eight structure formed by the connection of the 'new' Site C (discovered by magnetometry in 1994) with the ring-slots under Site A, excavated in 1961.

Navan Fort. If they do, it lies at the lowest point of the hill on the east, where a possible site might still be identified.

If an original entrance to the Navan enclosure lies in this sector, we can ignore the present entrance west of the mound, and the layout of the earthwork (which has been considered strangely tilted or awry on the hill) suddenly makes sense. A person or group entering the monument did so at the lowest point of the enclosure. Going up the hill in a straight line to the west, they had the most gradual ascent and travelled the longest distance within the enclosure. The flat summit and the mound were gradually revealed with theatrical effect, and the mound, arguably the goal of the progress, was silhouetted against a western sky (Fig 55). The fact that there was little room between the mound and the earthwork on the west did not matter. No one needed to go there.

Postscript

In 2002 a small excavation was carried out at a point on the downhill, eastern perimeter of the enclosure where the slope of the hillside and the geophysics suggested that the original entrance might lie. The point chosen for excavation lay at the lowest part of the enclosure, due east of the gap in the northern ring of Site C, and was flanked by parallel lines on the geophysics, possibly palisade slots connected with Site C. The bank had been levelled in recent centuries all along this

Fig. 55—The Navan mound approached uphill from the east, silhouetted against the western sky (photo: J. Finegan).

stretch, so there was no extant gap in the earthworks to focus on. The excavation on the line of the bank quickly revealed a sunken track paved with small stones. Unfortunately this did not appear to have been matched by a causeway across the ditch. Further survey and targeted geophysical investigations will help to resolve outstanding problems. Identifying the original entrance will enable discussion of the 'ceremonial dynamics' of the monument. For example, as noted above, if the entrance is indeed low down on the east, its site would correspond with the fact that the whole monument is tilted downhill in that direction.

Chapter 9

Towards an understanding

After all that has been uncovered and written about Navan Fort and the surrounding area over the last 40 years, are we any closer to working out why it was built? Certainly, we now know its age, but many in the 1950s might have guessed at a construction date of the first century BC on the basis that this was the date assigned to the legendary personages associated with it in the literature. Also, we know much more about ceremonial structures and activities in the sanctuary dating from its early first century BC heyday. But it is in the nature of the archaeological evidence for ritual that it often, as here, raises more questions than it solves.

We know from the destroyed megalithic tombs in Ballybrolly that the Navan area was of religious significance from the Late Neolithic period onwards. Haughey's Fort and the King's Stables, built in around 1000 BC, testify to wealth, prestige and continued ceremonial activity. Indeed, Jim Mallory has debated whether Haughey's Fort itself was in part a ceremonial monument or, as is usually supposed in the case of such hillforts, primarily a dwelling-place or secular and economic stronghold. The linear ditches in Creeveroe also suggest a ceremonial division in the landscape rather than a purely defence or stock boundary. A millennium later, the enclosure around Navan (the 'fort') was built, in the 90s BC, but we do not know what its relationship with Haughey's Fort was. There are remains of activity in Haughey's Fort during the Iron Age, but whether the site remained monumentally impressive or was occupied by (some of) the people who caused Navan Fort to be built is impossible to say. It is difficult to prove that Navan Fort was built where it was because of the existence of earlier monuments in the area. The existence, however, of a community, or even an institution, that demanded such a large ceremonial monument has to be presumed. All we can do is record the facts of its existence and date, point to the presence of older, possibly ceremonial, sites in the area and attempt in future research to find out what happened in the area during the millennium between the construction of Haughey's Fort and Navan Fort.

Having said that, we can presume that the site for the monument was not chosen whimsically by a group of wandering sanctuary-builders. Navan is not where it is because it was perceived as marginally better than a dozen other possible places. There would naturally have been much community debate and argument before people could have been persuaded or forced into such a large communal construction effort. The place must have already been of some importance, and this importance must have been widely recognised.

When I first worked on the Navan excavation as a student, I had conversations at lunchtime with Dudley Waterman, the rest of the excavation team and visitors to the excavation about what might be the significance of what we were digging up. There was no consensus, and most of the speculations did not fit well with the evidence. There was excitement in the excavation team at the discovery of something completely new, but there were concerns that the remains could not readily be interpreted in the light of discoveries made elsewhere. The feeling was that the facts should be recorded and published as thoroughly and objectively as possible and that others could worry later about what it all meant. After working on the dig in 1970, I could not avoid turning the story of the site over and over in my mind and trying to penetrate the 'meaning' or purpose behind the unique monumental structures. I bought a copy of Pronsias Mac Cana's *Celtic mythology* and other works on late prehistoric religion in Britain and Ireland in the hope that some plausible and comprehensive explanation for the Navan structures might emerge from a survey of pre-Christian beliefs. I hoped that some episode described in a myth or epic tale might plausibly have formed a model for the constructions that had recently been uncovered. I realised only later that such an approach made a number of assumptions that archaeologists and historians were not ready to accept, for example that there could be a relationship between tangible archaeological remains and mythic concepts. The brief survey of the secondary literature threw up no ready analogies for the Navan structures that might have led to an 'explanation' of them. I now believe, however, that, while *Celtic mythology* contains no specific reference to anything like the Navan structures, it may contain a whole chapter on what this site was designed for!

The excavation team was in general unconcerned with the religious background to the period or the type of site (in so far as it was then known) and preferred to maintain a detached objectivity in considering what it might be that they were uncovering. The discoveries being made at the site, however, were well known to Celtic scholars. Leading archaeologists in Iron Age studies, such as Ann Ross, visited the excavations and had lengthy discussions on site. No doubt, Dudley Waterman had plenty of suggestions about what it was that he was finding, but none of them took hold as the 'official' explanation. There was some evidence, indeed, that Waterman decided for the time being to avoid making any speculation about the specific significance of his discoveries. For example, we have seen that, when news spread about the large wooden 'ceremonial' structures that Bernard Wailes was finding in Knockaulin, Co. Kildare, in the early 1970s, Waterman stopped calling his Navan figure-of-eight Iron Age structures 'houses and baileys', preferring the more descriptive, less interpretative term 'southern and northern ring-slot enclosures'.

In the early 1990s the publication of the Navan excavations was in sight, and the question of the interpretation of the whole excavated sequence returned. The Department of the Environment could hardly publish a factual account of the excavation without at least attempting to offer an explanation for what had been found. The whole point of archaeological excavation is to provide data that can be used to fuel interpretation and to increase knowledge of how people lived, and, in the case of religious sites, to help understand beliefs at different times. In a process akin to thinking aloud about the Navan excavations, a series of articles appeared in *Emania* starting in 1992 that tried to grope towards an understanding of the monument. These essays have been greeted with the usual polite silence, so I cannot claim that there is any consensus about what is the 'true' or 'real' explanation for the extraordinary structures found by Waterman and his team in Navan.

I will summarise these thoughts below because they may help to stimulate readers' own ideas and because they chart the speculations of archaeologists closely involved with the material. I have adapted what follows to take account of new data (for example, we now know the age of the monument) and have omitted much material that now seems peripheral. This is also the place to issue a caution: bear in mind when considering some of the suggestions that most of what went before is fairly factual but what follows is mostly conjecture. The information from Navan for complex Iron Age religious ceremonial structures is unique in itself. But the accounts and deductions from literary sources about what may have been believed by people in the past in different areas of north-west Europe with which the Navan material must be compared are sometimes diverse, obscure and inconsistent. Some 'leaps of faith', generally unacceptable in scholarly discussion, are required if we are to get anywhere, and the best that we can hope for at the end is to be 'groping around in the right semantic areas', as one commentator put it. It seems best to begin the process by summarising again the core of what it is that we are trying to understand:

1. We have a large circular earthwork enclosure, a sanctuary defined by a ditch outside a bank built in the 90s BC, called Navan Fort and earlier known as Emain Macha.
2. In the bottom of the ditch at one point were several squared beams of oak that had been charred by fire on two opposite sides, evidently part of a large wooden structure that had partly burned.
3. The monument lies in an area where there were much older monuments. In the Neolithic period there were passage tombs, and in the Bronze Age there was a hillfort (Haughey's Fort) and other earthworks, some of which had a ceremonial character, including parallel linear ditches and an artificial pond (the King's Stables).
4. Also in the 90s BC a mound was built in a unique series of stages in the highest part of the sanctuary:
   - a large wooden building, 40m in diameter, formed of rings of large oak posts, was built;
   - a cairn, 2.5m high, of limestone blocks was placed inside the wooden structure;

the outer walls (at least) of the wooden structure were deliberately burned around the cairn;

the cairn was carefully covered with a layered mound of varied soils and turves.

5. Also in the 90s BC a series of large dykes (the Dorsey) was built across a routeway to Navan 25km to the south.

6. Other short lengths of linear earthworks (Black Pig's Dyke, Worm Ditch) were built at around the same time at places that could be considered as parts of a frontier zone.

7. Emain Macha was celebrated in the early medieval literature as the prehistoric royal capital of an ancient province (Ulster) of Ireland.

Given all this information, what more can we deduce about the significance of the place when it was constructed? Some might ask 'what more do you want to know?'. Surely the ancient tradition that Emain Macha was the Ulstermen's capital is all we need. Archaeology has outwardly revealed a surprising degree of correlation with aspects of the early traditions. There is a large enclosure, quite acceptable as a fort or stronghold in the eyes of medieval writers and early antiquarians. Excavation revealed evidence for high-status occupation (the Iron Age settlements of figure-of-eight structures, Phase 3). The date of this activity is very close to that claimed as the heyday of the site in the epics themselves. But there are significant inconsistencies between the tradition and the archaeology, which demand explanation outside the traditional view. The large enclosure is not a fort; it is a sanctuary, the circularity of its plan defining its sacred status. The positioning of the bank outside the ditch formed a boundary between the sacred inside and the profane outside. The mound was clearly a ceremonial structure, built in a series of pre-planned events, no doubt of great significance at the time. The building operations were presumably accompanied by ritual activities, including words and gestures that have left no traces. Navan Fort, therefore, was not a royal fort or military headquarters in 90 BC as portrayed in the tales. It was instead a religious and ceremonial centre of great significance. The fact that earthworks were built at around the same time across (some) routeways leading to the northern part of Ireland, roughly corresponding with the area of historical Ulster, suggests that the monuments at Navan and the ceremonials that took place there may have been of more than local significance.

One conclusion from this could be that the myths do not refer to this or any other physical place and that the ancient historians were wrong to tie them to Emain Macha. On this analysis we should not rely on the Ulster tales or other sources of early traditions to solve the archaeological problem of what was uncovered in Navan Fort. While K.H. Jackson argued in 1960 that the early tradition and the tales of the Ulster Cycle could be used with caution to provide a 'window on the Iron Age', some scholars have claimed that this is not the case. They point out that the Early Christian and medieval compilers, composers and redactors of the tales deliberately set them in a pre-Christian context to create Ireland's equivalent of the Biblical Old Testament. The writers could also have incorporated elements borrowed from a range of sources about pre-Christian traditions elsewhere (the Bible, Greek and Roman classics, Saxon and Scandinavian myth) to make their material appear to relate to a more remote time. Even the chariots used by the warriors in the Ulster Cycle could have been taken from the Greek epics. Putting the events of the tales into the last two centuries BC was only a device to bring it all neatly to a conclusion with the birth of Christ and thereby to reconcile the old with the new. On this view, the neat correlation between the dates of the archaeological remains at Navan and the other regional sanctuaries is only an unlucky coincidence. In any case, how could writers in the eighth century AD know anything about events that occurred a millennium earlier? How could genuine traditions have been preserved for centuries before writing was invented? T.F. O'Rahilly warned in his influential *Early Irish history and mythology* that 'the Otherworld is impervious to archaeological exploration'. He also observed that archaeologists often borrow uncritically from early histories to lend false credibility to their speculations.

I plan now to try to develop an understanding of the meaning of the ceremonial structures at Navan without reference to the early literary material because of the problems associated with its interpretation. We will at first approach the interpretation of the monuments as if there was no tradition about what may have happened in Emain Macha or pre-literate Ireland generally. We will try to rely entirely on the 'hard' archaeological evidence from the site itself and on the evidence for contemporaneous practices elsewhere.

The monuments
Clearly, the primary purpose of the Iron Age builders at Navan was to create three monuments (at least): the massive circular enclosure, the hilltop mound (Site B) and the large ring-barrow (Site A; its relationship to the other two monuments is as yet unclear, but it may be a little later in date). The profile (bank outside ditch) and the regular circularity of the outline of the main enclosure mean that we can confidently interpret it as the boundary of a sanctuary. From these same features of the monuments—size, regularity and the complexity of the design of the mound and the timber structure—we can also conclude that the community concerned had the advice of, or were controlled by, influential religious specialists. These specialists were probably aware of the existence of similar monuments and structures elsewhere and were able to demand considerable work from the community. The building of the monuments was carefully supervised in accordance with a specific design or a series of concepts. The overall design of the monuments was not dreamed by a single shaman in a trance. The complexity of the (puzzling) remains of the large ceremonial structures and the confidence of their construction testify to the existence of a codified set of religious beliefs informing the whole process.

Some of the most impressive ancient ceremonial monuments, such as megalithic tombs, survive today in relatively remote places. Their isolation, sometimes on inhospitable hilltops, may be one of the reasons why they have survived. But what about newly planned and built monuments, as these at Navan were in the 90s BC? New monuments are put in public places to be seen, to provide ongoing inspiration and to remind people of what they represent or memorialise. They were meant to be of use so that society was continually reminded of the events, personages or institutions that they celebrate and commemorate. Considerable community effort was invoked not simply to create a whimsical or symbolic folly, soon to be forgotten and deserted. The creation of ceremonial or commemorative monuments can be seen as an investment in the future and a statement of confidence. We can conclude, therefore, that, although there is little archaeological evidence for activity at Navan Fort after it and its central monuments were built, it was used, or at least was meant to be used, well into the future.

The size and form of the Navan earthworks suggest that they were of more than local significance. If they were 'local', that is, of significance only within the area immediately around the site, then there should be many other such sites elsewhere in the north of Ireland of about the same date—but we do not know of any (except the other regional ceremonial centres). If one small community needed such monuments, others would have as well. So far, archaeology has proved the existence of large circular Iron Age enclosures only at Navan, Tara and Knockaulin. Thus, the scale of the monuments, their layout, the lack of contemporaneous construction of similar sites (except at provincial centres) and the 'border' monuments of the same date (the Dorsey and Black Pig's Dyke) lead to the conclusion that the Navan sanctuary was of regional significance, that is, it was of significance to a people, a community of some sort, that occupied a large area. What that significance was, of course, is the key question.

There is no range of superficially comparable but anonymous sites in the countryside that on excavation might prove to be of the same class and date as these Iron Age monuments. A few comparable circular enclosures are known from elsewhere, for example the Giant's Ring near Belfast (Fig. 56), but when excavated many of these large earthwork enclosures of circular plan and lacking an external ditch have turned out to be of Neolithic date or certainly much older than the Iron Age. There seems to be little evidence at present that any large circular (ceremonial) earthwork enclosures were constructed between the Late Neolithic and the Iron Age. There is a gap in continuity of about 1000 years between the construction of hillforts like Haughey's Fort and the Navan sanctuary. Why did people suddenly build these closely comparable monuments and complex wooden structures at widely separated sites (Navan, Tara, Knockaulin and (probably) Cruachan)? This remarkable phase of monumental standardisation and ceremonial activity suggests that in around 100 BC there was some form of ideological unity over a large area of Ireland. This may seem like an elementary conclusion, but it is not an assumption that can be made regarding prehistory. For example, the regionalised distribution of various types of megalithic monuments suggests that there were differences in beliefs and ceremonial practices from one area to another in the Neolithic and the Bronze Age. But we can go further. Not only was there a degree of ideological consensus, but it appears that it was expressed monumentally at a few widely scattered sites. This suggests that Ireland may have been divided into several regions, each with one of these monument complexes as a focus for ceremonies.

The purpose of the Navan sanctuary
The purpose of the large enclosure at Navan, the 'sanctuary', is perhaps the easiest

Fig. 56—Aerial view of the Giant's Ring, Ballynahatty, south of Belfast.

to assess initially. The large earthwork defined a special area, arguably a sacred space. As we noted earlier, such a large monument was hardly built to be ignored. Presumably the people, or some of them, intended to use it continuously or periodically for some purpose important to the well-being of the community. I say 'periodically' because there is not, as yet, any evidence that the place continued to be permanently or seasonally occupied after the visible monuments were built. Further evidence for continuing occupation might yet turn up. If the pre-mound occupation layers had been ploughed, as would any later settlement area in the enclosure not covered by the mound, the evidence for the relatively shallow figures of eight would have been removed, and we would be left with only a scatter of crumbly pottery and some glass beads. The metal objects would probably have rotted completely in the topsoil. Another possibility is that, when the monument was 'used' after its construction, any contemporaneous settlement of the 'custodians' of the place would have been outside the ring. Also, it is possible that, if other people came to the site for purposes of ceremony, gatherings or veneration, they remained generally outside it. Evidence for extra-mural religious or ceremonial activity is provided by the deposition of the bronze horns in nearby Loughnashade. This shows that the hill of Navan, with its enclosures and mound, was not the only place in the landscape that had spiritual significance in the Iron Age.

The hilltop mound of Site B presents a unique problem. Why would any group build a large circular building, pile a cairn of stones inside it and set it on fire? This mound, with its contemporaneous enclosure (the 'Fort'), was one of the last large-scale pagan ceremonial monuments of Europe outside the classical world. The people who built Navan are unlikely to have been aware that the ancient ways were going to come to an end. As far as they knew, life and culture on the large island at the western tip of Europe were going to continue much as they had done, evolving relatively gently in response to internal pressures, external influences, settlers and trade, and with their language(s), customs and institutions continuing relatively unperturbed. The Navan structures were built at a time relatively close to the beginning of real history, much nearer to us in time than megalithic tombs, for example. We expect, therefore, that the ideology underlying their construction could be deduced by putting the evidence from the site itself alongside what we know about the beliefs and ceremonial activities, at a community level, of the peoples of western Europe at the time. We have material evidence for certain actions, and we can call on contemporaneous commentators and, even better, eyewitness evidence for similar things elsewhere.

Later prehistoric and traditional beliefs

We have little direct evidence from Iron Age Ireland about what people may have believed, apart from that contained in the very sites we are trying to interpret. There are no contemporaneous records, no inscriptions and no images, apart from a few

Fig. 57—Iron Age pattern carved on a stone built into a church at Derrykeighan, Co. Antrim.

interesting stones carved with abstract curvilinear decoration (Fig. 57). The date, provenance and meaning of a few carved stone figures, arguably of Early Iron Age date, are too problematic to allow them a pivotal contribution to a general assessment of an Iron Age ideology (Fig. 58).

In Britain 'Romano-Celtic' temples, built after the middle of the first century AD, were sometimes pre-dated by wooden Iron Age structures, which, from their positions, were presumably also used for religious purposes in the pre-Roman Iron Age. Offerings of precious objects were made in rivers, like the famous shields from the River Thames. These remind us of the deposition of the horns in Loughnashade and of similar precious objects like the Broighter Hoard from near Limavady, Co. Londonderry. In the absence, however, of contemporaneous inscriptions or

Fig. 58—The 'Tandragee Figure', a prehistoric 'idol', now in Armagh Cathedral.

iconography (graphic depictions of religious themes, incidents or personages), it is impossible to work out, except in rather general terms, what meanings lay behind the structures in major archaeological sites and offerings in bogs and lakes. But we can be sure that, when people in the past carried out a ceremony or made an offering of costly objects, the act was deeply charged with meaning and was expected to have a beneficial outcome. Religious ideology was not a vague set of obscure ideas to the people who carried out or attended the rites to which archaeology bears witness. The deposition of metalwork or the construction of large monuments can be presumed, in the minds of those making the offerings and building the structures, to have had immediate and longer-term desirable effects.

Some general insights into these ideas and purposes might be given by a brief review of the beliefs of 'traditional societies' and how early historic peoples in Europe may have interacted with their spiritual world. This can only be superficial compared with the more scientific processes of 'comparative religion', but a review may help us to get into the mindset or world-view of a traditional society that may to some extent overlap with what was going on in the minds of Iron Age people in the north of Ireland. That said, there may be some universality in the way that humankind reacts to and manages religious experiences and ceremonies. Religious rites tend to repeat archetypal events performed in a remote time, or before time began, by ancestors or gods. In this way, people gave reality and relevance to everyday actions like cooking or farming. The actions could be turned into ceremonies in line with the archetypes performed by the gods at the dawn of creation. People of many ancient or traditional societies tried to live as much as possible in the realm of the sacred or close to sacred objects. The sacred was the ultimate power and reality. For many cultures, the discovery of a fixed point, the centre, was equivalent to the foundation and creation of the world. Traditional peoples' desire to live in the sacred, or, in their view, objective reality, gave rise to techniques for the construction of sacred spaces. The rituals used in the construction of sacred spaces frequently replicated the work of the gods, that is, the mythology of the society. The most important structures repeated the 'cosmogony', that is, the creation myth of the people concerned.

Rituals were closely related to the calendar. Time was imagined as being reborn each new year, cleansed of all the misfortunes of the previous year. New time had the sanctity it originally received from 'the creator' renewed. The year was imagined as a closed circle but with a beginning and an end, a concept that can find expression in the architecture of temples, circuses and sanctuaries. Rebirth of time at the beginning of the new year was brought about by recitation or re-enactment of creation myths. The new year festival, therefore, was not just a commemoration; it re-enacted the cosmogony, the model of creation. The circular plan of Navan Fort, the concentric timber circles and the westward orientation of the wooden structure in the mound may have been intended in part to symbolise these or related concepts. An overwhelming majority of ancient circular structures in Ireland and Britain faced east, toward the rising sun and away from the wet westerly winds. The Navan wooden structure faced due west, toward the setting sun at around the time of the autumn equinox, clearly in a conscious reversal of the normal orientation. Perhaps this orientation is explained by the fact that some of the ancient peoples of Europe believed that the day began at sunset. Whatever the precise intention behind the unusual westerly orientation, it seems to link the structure with time or the calendar.

We noted earlier that ceremonial structures and sanctuaries were often built at places identified by traditional societies as sacred centres. The concept of the centre was sometimes emphasised by the image of a universal cosmic pillar, the *axis mundi*, which stood at the centre of the earth (as far as the people who recognised it were concerned), and the entire habitable world extended around it. The *axis mundi*, which could be a pillar, a post or even a sacred tree, also had a role in reconciling the three cosmic realms: it connected the heavens with the surface of the earth, and its base was fixed below ground. It is hard to avoid the conclusion that some such role was assigned to the large post, like a totem pole, that formed the focus of the Navan multi-ring timber structure. The building may have been deliberately designed like a mandala to enable procession along the three aisles and around the post rings to venerate the post at the centre.

The idea that the wooden building may have been used internally, even briefly, as part of its construction ritual, for some ceremonial purpose evokes the architectural concept we sometimes describe by the word 'temple'. Perhaps the wooden building and the entire sanctuary formed a 'temple' or a structure that shared in the attributes of a temple. The cosmological design of a temple provided an earthly representation of a transcendental heavenly model. According to Mircea Eliade, the temple continually re-sanctified the world because it both represented and contained it. If the Navan structures represented 'the world', what was that world like? At the centre of the world was a monumental mound, which itself contained a model or image of something else, probably of cosmological significance. Around the sacred mound was an open grassy area, falling away in all directions. Possibly this represented the world inhabited by the builders of the sanctuary and those who revered it. Beyond that was a large earthwork boundary or enclosure: a deep ditch with an external bank. This may have symbolised the limits of the world inhabited by those who recognised the sanctuary as a sort of capital. The curving linear earthworks built at various places in the north of Ireland (such as the Dorsey) at around the same time as Navan Fort may also have been erected by the group responsible for building Navan. If this was the case, the Navan earthworks could indeed be interpreted as a world model, that world having earthworks at its borders, represented on a smaller scale by the banks of the sanctuary. On the other hand, the construction of earthworks at the periphery of a territory may have been triggered by the desire to expand to a regional scale the exemplary design of the earthworks at the sacred centre. The role of Site A, however, in such a scheme is problematic, although we do not yet know if it was built at the same time as the other monuments. Pursuing this flight of fancy, however, we might speculate that Loughnashade may have symbolised the watery domain, which was partly within the region (rivers and lakes) and partly enclosed it (the sea, if we consider that the whole of the north of Ireland was the territory concerned).

There seems little doubt that the creation of sacred space formed an important element in the construction of the earthworks and mound at Navan Fort. It has been suggested that, since celestial geometry is believed to have made the first constructions possible and to have provided their architectural inspiration, the structures themselves shared in the sacrality of the skies. Perhaps some such concept provides a background for the skyward-facing geometry of the timber building and the radial alignments on the cairn surface.

Another feature that would be expected in the inauguration of a new 'temple' is the ritual of sanctification. Sometimes this involved a blood sacrifice to transfer a 'soul' to the structure. In this context, we recall that a small but strangely representative collection of animal bones and a human clavicle (Fig. 59) came from among the Navan cairn stones. The process of sanctification may also have been completed by incineration, for which there is plentiful evidence from the mound. Some rituals of construction repeated the cosmogony, the exemplary acts of the gods of which the world was born, for example by dismemberment of the body of a primordial giant. We will return to this theme.

A normal 'fort' has its bank uphill, inside the ditch. In this configuration the defenders on the top of the bank have the greatest height advantage over the attackers, who have to struggle across the ditch and up the face of the bank, all the while potentially under missile attack. The position is reversed at Navan Fort: with the bank downslope from the ditch, it looks as if the defenders are on the outside. Unlike the Neolithic henge enclosures, Navan Fort has a very deep, V-sectioned ditch, which does indeed have defensive characteristics. Perhaps the sanctuary can be imagined as a container for the spiritual forces that could only be accessed within.

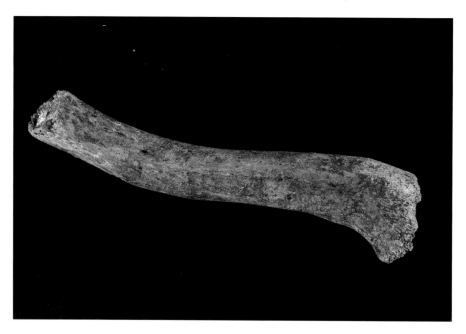

Fig. 59—Clavicle from a young man found among the cairn stones of the Site B mound.

This may seem to contradict the earlier suggestion that traditional peoples liked to live in the sacred, but it may be that the earthworks were meant to generate or enshrine something more specific, which was not regarded as a suitable component of everyday life. Richard Warner has suggested in *Emania* that the mound may have been regarded as a portal to the Otherworld and that the surrounding earthwork was designed to prevent the Otherworld forces there released from spilling out into this world.

Contemporaneous accounts of religious beliefs

So far, we have looked at Navan and the structures uncovered there as isolated finds and have tried to interpret them in the light of suggestions drawn from the field of comparative religion. We are not, however, without witnesses to the beliefs and rituals of the peoples of north-west Europe in the last few centuries BC. There is the evidence of the excavation of other ceremonial sites, which testifies to the widespread use of cult sites. Even more significant are the views of reliable witnesses, like Posidonius, a Greek ethnographer of the early first century BC whose lost works were widely quoted in Julius Caesar's *Gallic Wars* and by the historian Tacitus. These works have been the subject of detailed analysis that need not be repeated here. There are many comprehensive books on the subject of what is sometimes called 'Celtic religion' as exemplified by archaeological finds, ceremonial sites, descriptions from the classical world, Gaulish iconography, inscriptions and motifs from medieval Irish sources. These last sources are sometimes the tales of the Ulster Cycle centred on Navan Fort, but I am attempting to reach some understanding of what Navan Fort was meant to symbolise or what function it was designed to perform without, at first, using this material. The frequent use of the term 'Celtic religion' implies some form of ideological unity across the lands inhabited by speakers of Celtic languages (so grouped in relatively recent times) at different times in the past. While this may be true to some extent, the term in my view does not sufficiently allow for changes with time and for local and regional variations and cults. There is also the likelihood that major elements of the religion of Celtic speakers were not confined to them.

It may seem strange to avoid using traditions and lore that explicitly refer to the very site we are trying to understand. This, as we have seen, is because of the possibility that the later sources contain much that was composed anew in the medieval period to underpin ideas current only at that time. It has even been suggested that the *Táin* itself was a conscious imitation of the *Iliad* or that some of the early mythological material embedded in the tales was brought to Ireland by immigrants displaced by the Roman conquest of Britain. In reacting to overenthusiastic acceptance of the truth of the early sources, some modern commentators have gone so far in the other direction as to deny that the early literature could have any relevance to prehistoric times. We will return to this question but in the meantime will try to make constructive use of Continental and British evidence for (seemingly relevant) religious ideas at the same time as Navan was constructed. The Roman commentators make it clear that the way of life of the Britons and their beliefs about the gods were similar to those of the Gauls, and

Tacitus wrote that the inhabitants of Ireland had a similar culture to the Britons.

When we go through a summary of what happened when the Navan mound was constructed—build a huge wooden building (possibly a model of something else), put a cairn of stones inside it and burn both as part of a ceremonial offering—an eerie feeling dawns that this description is vaguely familiar. Could it be that the Navan sequence of monument building is a variation on the extraordinary ritual carried out (allegedly) on behalf of Gaulish states and described by one of the most famous figures of the ancient world, Julius Caesar? Incorporating the works of the Greek philosopher and ethnographer Posidonius, he described how some of the Gaulish tribes, in carrying out sacrifices on behalf of the state, made colossal images of wickerwork, filled them with living victims and set the structure alight (Fig. 60). The Navan mound was constructed in a series of stages that seem to provide a monumental analogy with the 'wickerman' rite. There was a large wooden building, arguably a cosmic model, something was packed inside (stones), and the structure was deliberately set on fire. Bruce Lincoln has recently studied the significance of the 'wickerman' sacrifice. He called it a 'mesocosm', a halfway house between humans, the microcosm and the cosmos itself. Lincoln has drawn out and codified what he presents as the ancients' understanding of how the world was created and maintained in being. The world was created from the body of a primordial giant, one

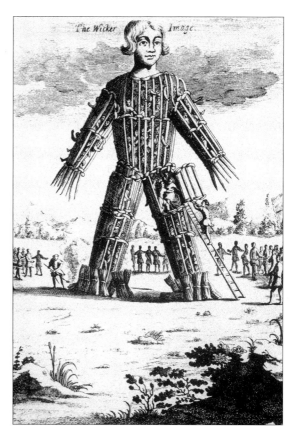

Fig. 60—'The enormous wooden image' described by Caesar as imagined in the seventeenth century by Aylett Sammes.

of twins. One of the twins was a priest who sacrificed and dismembered the body of the other twin (who was the first king) to create the world. Outlandish as this suggestion appears, the names of some of these twins have passed into more sanitised epics and pseudo-history and are familiar to us today, for example in the Roman tradition as Romulus and Remus (who was killed by Romulus) and in the Saxon tradition as Hengist and Horsa.

The ancient creation myth explained that not only was the world made from the parts of a 'twin' but so also were the three main social classes of the ancient world, the priests from his head, the warriors from his arms and torso, and the provider classes from his waist and legs. So the cosmogonic myth also neatly contained the story of how human society itself came about. According to Lincoln, a dynamic relationship, which by sacrifice could be maintained in balance, was believed to exist between the world of humans and the cosmos. A deterioration in one could be redressed by sacrificing part of the other to redress the balance. This, he concluded, was the reason for the mass sacrifice implied by the classical description of the wickerman. While the analogy with the Navan mound should not be overworked, the idea of the dynamic between humans and the cosmos could be valuable in furthering our understanding. Just as parts of society were imagined to have come from specific parts of the primordial twin, so too did specific parts of the material world, the cosmos. Stones were equated with bones, soil with flesh, water with blood, thoughts with clouds, vegetation with hair, and so on. Viewed in this light, the Navan mound may have another significance as a collection and symbolic reassembly of these cosmic materials to produce a composition of much greater significance than the separate components.

The ancient European societies from which these religious analogies come were ruled by kings, often local 'tribal' kings, many of whom may have given allegiance to an over-king of a much greater area. Some have suggested that, because of the gap in time between the construction of Navan Fort and the beginning of history, speculation about the system of governance in Iron Age Ireland is a complete waste of time. But when history began Ireland was ruled by hundreds of tribal kings. This system of government is of very remote antiquity, and there is no valid alternative system that might have operated in Iron Age Ireland. The Old Irish word for king, *rí*, is cognate with Gaulish *rix*, 'king', and Latin *rex*, 'king'. It is a term inherited from Indo-European *$r\bar{e}g$- and was brought to Ireland by the earliest Celtic speakers. To suggest that the rulers of Iron Age Ireland were 'kings' in the general sense of what that institution constituted elsewhere in western Europe at the same time (as described in the classical sources) is not as unsound as projecting back into the past some specific description from a medieval epic.

Chapter 10

Macha and kingship

Macha: a tri-functional goddess

In 1968 the celebrated French comparative mythologist Georges Dumézil wrote: 'To judge from what remains of Emain Macha in Ireland...and from many other sites it is hard to imagine that there existed in these Celtic countries a body of Druids whose studies—theology, ritual, law and epic traditions—lasted up to twenty years. Over how many archaeological excavations does not one experience the same astonishment?'. Dumézil contrasted the bleak humps and bumps of archaeological sites with the richness of historical testimony and literary tradition originating in the same times and cultures. It is not surprising that he should first mention Emain Macha as one of the sites most likely to preserve evidence of Druidic learning. It is unlikely, however, despite his references to archaeological excavations, that Dumézil was aware of what was then being uncovered in Navan Fort. If he had, I do not believe he would have been so astonished. I suspect, rather, that he would have been fascinated and intrigued. In 1954 he had written an article, 'Le trio des Macha', in which he pointed out that the three legends about the goddess after which Navan Fort/Emain Macha is named single her out as a prime example of a 'tri-functional goddess'.

One of Dumézil's achievements was to have identified a pattern often reflected in the mythological themes of the scattered Indo-European peoples that became known as 'the tripartite ideology'. In short, this is manifest by a tendency to group certain concepts in hierarchical groups of three. Primarily, according to Dumézil, this reflected the consistent stratified order of society itself in different places and times, including Vedic India, the Slavic lands, Rome and the places occupied by Germanic and Celtic-speaking peoples. The idealised society reflected in myth had: at the top, a small number of priests and lawmakers; in the middle, a larger group of warriors or people concerned with the legitimate exercise of force on behalf of the community; and, at the bottom, the biggest group, the farmers and providers, who supported the physical well-being of the whole community. We noted the existence of this hierarchical social grouping earlier when the ancient creation myth was mentioned. The values or activities represented by these groups were abstracted by Dumézil into three 'functions', the uppermost (F1) relating to religion and law, the middle (F2) armed force, and the lowermost (F3) fertility and productivity. These themes have been amplified, elaborated and identified in many mythological motifs by Dumézil, his contemporaries and his followers. Some have suggested that the ideological tripartition is much more pervasive and is not primarily connected with the social order. Some have said that it does not exist, that it is not restricted to Indo-Europeans or that it is simply a recognition of a more general human tendency to think that way.

Dumézil pointed out that there were three Machas in legend, or rather three legends about the one Macha of this site. The first Macha was the wife of Nemhed (the 'sacred one'); she died in one of the twelve plains of Ireland cleared by her husband; and it was for this reason that the plain around Emain was called after her (some scholars accept that the word 'Macha' is derived from *mag*, a 'plain'). Sanctity, the clearing of land and giving names are all first-function activities and relate to the sovereignty of the region concerned. The second Macha was the warrior queen who defeated the sons of Dithorba, who attempted to cheat her of her inheritance, the 'kingship' of Ireland, determined by her father. She marked out the boundaries of Emain Macha with her neck-brooch and forced the vanquished brothers to build it. This Macha clearly represents the second function, (military) force deployed in just defence of the realm. The third Macha was the supernatural bride of a mortal farmer, to whom she brought additional wealth and a pair of twins. Her husband's boasts about her qualities at a royal gathering in Emain resulted in her being forced to race against the king's horses. This Macha was interpreted by Dumézil as a third-function representative on the basis of her wealth-giving and fertility attributes.

This material is interesting, but has it any relevance to the present enquiry into the intentions of the builders of Navan Fort and the ceremonial structures inside it? Is there any possibility that Macha or some such personage was associated with the site when it was built? Until recently, it would have been silly to pose this question because we did not know the date of the monument. It could have dated from the Bronze Age or even the Neolithic, times so remote in the past that traditions connected with the original purposes of the place could not be expected to have survived. But we now know that Navan was completed in the 90s BC, (only) 500 or 600 years before the time when solid traditions about the site can be said to have emerged from the mists of prehistory. It is a long time, but not as long as a millennium. It is perhaps a period over which some traditions concerning the original significance of the place may have survived. As far as we know, there was no major invasion of the area, displacement of population or imposition of a new language that might have caused a sudden break with the builders' tradition. The builders of Navan Fort spoke a Celtic language, which evolved into the Old Irish current in the area at the beginning of history. There is no reason to argue for social and religious amnesia at a community level or for a learned cover-up, at least until the coming of Christianity.

The designers and builders of Navan Fort set out one day in the 90s BC (or whatever date they reckoned it to be—a certain year of a king's reign?) to mark out the perimeter of their new monument. They did *not* arbitrarily decide to build a 'class 4 henge with a tumulus' on some hitherto anonymous and unremarkable drumlin. They had decided to build a large sanctuary, on a special hill, for a particular purpose, perhaps even dedicated to a particular personage. They also built a large mound inside the sanctuary, which also had a specific purpose or purposes. These remains, which have been elaborated by archaeological excavation, are contemporaneous documents for Iron Age religious beliefs.

The early accounts of Emain Macha do not weld two conflicting traditions particularly well. We know that the site is described in the tales of the Ulster Cycle as a warrior headquarters, like an Ulster Troy or Camelot. Some descriptions of the site in the tales make it sound much as it does now: grassy banks, a mound and a surrounding plain. These traditions could have been imposed on the site at any time, the storytellers interpreting a long-abandoned ancient monument as a fort, much as it appeared in their day. At the time when the traditional lore was first being written down and/or composed as literary works, the well-to-do, the people listening to the tales, were living in small circular earthwork enclosures averaging 40–50m in internal diameter, which we now call raths or ringforts. It was perfectly natural for the members of such a society to think that a huge enclosure such as Navan Fort was the royal residence of an important king (even if the bank and ditch are the 'wrong' way round). If, however, there was no inherited tradition about the site in the Early Christian period, why (using names borrowed from contemporaneous 'legends') was it not called Dún Conchobar or Ráth Deirdre, for example? It seems certain that the early writers had inherited some core of tradition, even just the place-name associating the site with Macha, that could not be suppressed or explained away. There is a possibility that the monument was indeed dedicated to the personage identified in the early literature as the local territorial goddess, Macha, when it was first built.

It is interesting to speculate that the idea of living in small circular enclosures in Early Christian Ireland was inherited from an Iron Age ideology. This is a reversal of the idea that rath-dwellers in the Early Christian period assumed that the ancient circular sanctuaries were ancient forts. The small raths may have been primarily intended to define monumentally the sacred area of hearth and home. The earthworks may have had positive or negative effects on the drainage of the small settlement, but they could not have provided significant defence. While they may have improved management of the dwelling area by excluding stock, for example, they did not do anything that wooden fences and hedges achieved in other periods. The circular raths may be related ideologically to the larger circular enclosures defining the sanctuary areas of early ecclesiastical sites, thereby providing another ideological link with Iron Age circular sanctuaries and ring-barrows.

Navan and the 'five fifths'
I now leave the attempt to develop an understanding of Navan Fort based mainly on

archaeological findings and contemporaneous observations of the ways of the Continental Gauls and others. I turn to draw on some aspects of what has been termed the 'Insular tradition'. This is a body of literary material, some of which is alleged to come from an oral tradition in Ireland, pre-dating the advent of writing, which had the potential to preserve facts and opinions forever. According to the earliest 'histories', Ireland in prehistoric times was divided into five provinces or over-kingdoms known as the 'five fifths'. The early Irish word for 'province' is *cóiced*, a 'fifth'. The five provinces were Ulster, Leinster, Munster and Connacht, with Meath in the middle. According to Alwyn and Brinley Rees, the middle province was a microcosm of the whole island, which thus seems to have been conceived of, at one level, as a cosmological unity. Each of the five provinces had a recognised headquarters: Meath, Tara; Ulster, Emain Macha; Leinster, Dún Ailinne, Co. Kildare; Connacht, Cruachan, Co. Roscommon; and Munster, Dinn Ríg (whereabouts uncertain), later replaced by Cashel. Other ceremonial sites were recognised, and in an alternative scheme, proposed by Geoffrey Keating, they appear to have represented the surrounding provinces within Meath. Thus Tailtiu (Teltown) was associated with Ulster, Tlachta with Munster, Uisneach with Connacht and Tara with Leinster (Fig. 61).

One theme links the names of all these sites: they are all called after goddesses who are reputedly buried in or near the sites dedicated to them; for example, Macha is linked with Emain Macha, Medb with Tara and Cruacha with Cruachan. All of the major provincial sites are associated with kingship and are often referred to as 'the royal sites'. Periodically, special gatherings were held at them, for example the annual *feis* of Tara at which the legitimacy of the ruling king of the province of Meath was re-established. Here we finally get to the core of the issue. Emain Macha and the other Irish 'royal sites' are said to have been used by the regional communities for the inauguration of kings and the periodic reaffirmation of legitimate rulership. The subject of ancient kingship opens up a vast panorama of interrelated studies that in summary would fill several books. In connection with Navan Fort I will explore a few concepts associated with early kingship that may be relevant to the monumental remains we seek to understand.

Kingship

In the early historic period there were over a hundred kings in Ireland. Generally they were kings of small territories, subsidiary kings of small population groups, which it would be inaccurate to describe as clans or tribes. These lesser kings recognised over-kings and even kings of provinces who had managed to establish control over areas bigger than their personal kingdoms. The provincial kingship of Ulster survived only as an ideal, as no one in the early historic period was able to make himself king over the whole of the north of Ireland. Yet a consistent tradition looked back to a time in prehistory when people believed that the whole province, which had little real meaning in the early historic period, was once united under the kings of the Ulaidh, who ruled from Emain Macha. This belief was so powerful that it influenced political aspirations and underlay repeated attempts to recreate the ancient polity. The strength of the tradition was used to justify the expansionist

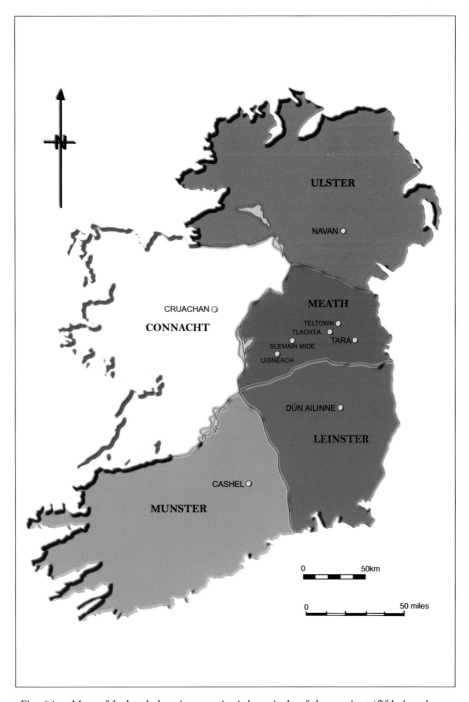

Fig. 61—Map of Ireland showing provincial capitals of the ancient 'fifths' and significant Meath sites. The provinces have been coloured in accordance with their cosmological characteristics: white: sacred, red: warfare, blue: productivity, green: goddess.

exploits of some early historic kings. But can this idea of a united Ulster ruled from Emain Macha, which seems to be accepted by eminent historians, have gone back as far as the Early Iron Age? All we can say is, well, what could have changed in the meantime? Early Irish kingship has many aspects that testify to a very archaic, Indo-European origin for the institution. If this tradition was not inherited from a remote prehistory within Ireland (at least as far back as the first or second century BC), where could it have come from instead?

Tacitus, the Roman historian, tells us that in AD 82 Agricola, the Roman governor of Britain, met an Irish prince who had been expelled because of a rebellion. Agricola hoped to get useful information from him in case the Romans decided to invade Ireland. Tacitus also says that in soil and climate, and in the character and civilisation of its inhabitants, Ireland was much like Britain. Ptolemy of Alexandria, a Greek geographer of the first century AD, was mentioned earlier. He gave coordinates and names of places, capes, rivers and peoples that can be turned into a map of Britain and Ireland (Fig. 62). The accuracy of this information bears out the statement of Tacitus that the approaches and harbours of Ireland were well known from the reports of merchants who traded there. Ptolemy mentioned places such as the mouth of the River Lagan and a people who lived in north-east Ireland called Voluntii, clearly an earlier version of the word for the Ulaidh, the early historic people who claimed to have ruled the area in earlier times. Ptolemy recorded a place called Isamnion, which some have claimed may be Navan. He also mentioned two inland places called Regia, one of which, from its location, might be Emain Macha or Clogher, Co. Tyrone. *Regia* means 'royal palace' or 'king's house', suggesting that the institution of kingship was important in the Ireland of the first century AD, only a century after Navan Fort was built.

St Patrick, writing in the fifth century AD, says that he encountered many kings and druids, which suggests that a non-Roman and essentially prehistoric system of royal government existed in his time. Another backward link is provided by some lines in the early seventh-century poem or hymn to St Patrick written by Fiacc, a monk of Armagh. The poet says: 'In Armagh there is the kingship, it has long since forsaken Emain, In the past the tribes worshipped the *síd*, they now worship the true Trinity.' There is no evidence that the ideology that underlay the institution of kingship at the very beginning of the historic period had changed much since the time when Navan Fort was built.

The inauguration of early historic Irish kings may hold some valuable clues to understanding the role that Navan Fort and similar sites may have played in early ceremonials. The king was usually selected from a royal dynasty. There was not direct succession from father to son: in theory all the males descended from a common great-grandfather were eligible. The king designate, the *tánaiste*, was sometimes chosen during the lifetime of his royal predecessor, but there were frequent disputes and much bloodshed over the succession. At the moment of his inauguration the candidate was imagined as becoming an entirely different person—a king. The king was a microcosm of society, and he was meant to represent all its aspects and to dispense justice fairly to all. Whatever his previous background, he became at once a judge and war-leader and a guarantor of

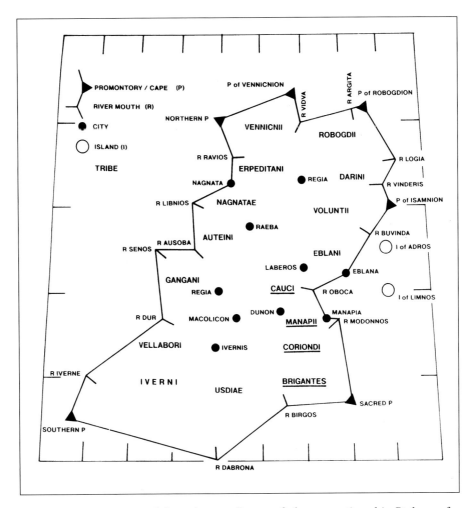

Fig. 62—Map constructed from the coordinates of places mentioned in Ptolemy of Alexandria's gazetteer (Emania 9, cover).

economic well-being. He acquired a new persona as a 'tri-functional' person, and it appears that he acquired this quality, known as *flaith*, in the process of inauguration by his symbolic wedding with the tri-functional goddess. This may be one reason why the association of Macha with this particular archaeological site is so significant.

In some sources the 'sovereignty' goddess is portrayed as the instrument that identifies the person who would rightfully become king and that would bestow on him his tri-functional nature. Irish sovereignty lore has repeated examples of this theme. Accounts of the inauguration of kings in early historic times demonstrate the continuance of this concept, even if its meaning was not fully appreciated. When he was inaugurated, the king was given three symbolic gifts: a white shirt symbolising the sacred, a wand of office symbolising his authority, and a shoe filled with grain or money symbolising wealth. In ancient India the equivalent garment was a cap soaked in sacred butter (*gee*), which filled the role of a crown. It is interesting that the distribution of the gifts (headgear symbolising the sacred, which is transcendent and above, a weapon held in the arms and a shoe put on the foot) corresponds with the parts of the body of the first king, from which the respective orders of society (priests, warriors and producers) were supposed to have sprung. Each newly inaugurated king took the place of the first king, who had been sacrificed and dismembered by his brother, the first priest. Indeed, some sources suggest that each succeeding king may have been thought of as ruling jointly with the first king.

Having established the likelihood that Navan Fort, as one of the provincial 'royal sites' of Ireland, is to be understood in terms of provincial kingship ceremonies, I do not want to explore further the question of ancient kingship. The enquiry would be overwhelmed in an attempt to do justice to the subject. We will finally look at some specific aspects of the site that might be better understood in the light of ancient kingship lore. The first element of the name of the monument, *Emain*, has been explained in several ways. For example, the medieval *Dinnsenchus* ('lore of places') explains the term as *eo muin*, the neck-brooch with which Macha in one of her legends is said to have marked out the monument for her captives to dig, much as Romulus is said to have marked out the *pomerium* of the first Rome with a plough. Another explanation, which might better fit the ideas developing here, is that it may mean 'twin'. Compare the words for twin: Old Irish *emon*, Latin *geminus* and Indo-European **yem-ono*. If the name of the site meant 'twin' coupled with the name of a tri-functional goddess, it would be difficult to think of two words, twin and goddess, that more completely encapsulate the concepts underlying early kingship ideology.

Inauguration sites
It is clear that many places used for the inauguration of kings in early historic and medieval Ireland were natural sites with a good view or were mounds that were already ancient. We do not know that any ancient inauguration sites were built specifically for that purpose, although archaeological excavation might reveal relevant evidence in the future. Some medieval inauguration sites had stone 'chairs', usually natural slabs forming a seat; others had a pair of footprints carved in a boulder. Among the purposes of inauguration were the need to integrate the king with the landscape and the people he would rule and to affirm his intention that he would rule according to traditions stretching back in unbroken succession to the first person who filled that particular office. A new monument would hardly fit with the ideology of the ceremony. For example, in the Middle Ages the O'Connors were inaugurated at Carnfree, a small kerbed mound some distance from the main group of prehistoric earthworks at Rathcroghan, Co. Roscommon. The O'Neills were inaugurated in a stone chair near an earthwork at Tullahoge, a village near Cookstown, Co. Tyrone. The O'Donnells were inaugurated on a prominent natural rock at Kilmacrenan, Co. Donegal, and the Maguires on what seems to have been a Neolithic passage tomb at Cornashee (the 'cairn of the fairies') near Lisnaskea, Co. Fermanagh. The use of ancient monuments would have underlined the people's title

to the place, as they could be imagined as symbolising the works and perhaps even containing the graves of their royal ancestors. But the suggestion here is that Navan Fort (enclosure and mound), Ráth na Ríogh at Tara and Knockaulin, Co. Kildare (enclosure only), were built or refurbished at around the same time to be used in kingship ceremonials.

Whether or not this is correct, the building of large and similar-looking earthworks and timber structures at sites later identified as prehistoric provincial centres suggests that the political geography of a large part of Ireland at the top level was being organised and institutionalised according to an overall plan. Otherwise, why should similar and arguably coordinated construction happen at the same time at key sites identified 600 years later as ancient provincial capitals? This does not necessarily mean that the island was ruled in a coordinated way. It is more likely that the religious establishment and local advisors had achieved a degree of common purpose and may have influenced their respective rulers to consolidate and assert their power on a regional basis. Part of the process may have involved constructing similar ceremonial monuments designed to give future stability and identity to the institutions they represented.

Are there any aspects of the structures found in Navan Fort that seem to align specifically with kingship ceremonial? The primary monument in the enclosure was the big mound. Kings are often associated with mounds in mythology. Often, mounds are portrayed as covering the dwellings or royal courts of Otherworld kings such as Midir, who bore Etáin off to Síd Breg Léith. In Welsh myth, kings are often associated with mounds. Pwyll, lord of Dyfed, sat on a throne-mound and had a vision of his future bride. In the *Táin bó Cuailgne* Conchobar and his troops set up a camp on the eve of the decisive battle at Slemain Mide. Conchobar reviewed his detachments of troops from the top of a mound of turves built for him by the men he reviewed 'because it is right that a king of a province should sit on a mound of turves'. The idea of a king sitting on a mound, however, could have arisen from the use of mounds elsewhere during the Early Christian period for similar purposes, rather than from an inherited memory of an Iron Age ceremony. The same applies to Giolla Brighde Mac Con Midhe's thirteenth-century poetic vision of the inauguration of a king in Emain Macha. The poet imagined that four warrior hosts converged on Emain from north, south, east and west, ground their weapons on the hill, gathered round the mound and 'the poetbands of the world made Roalbh from the rath of Conchobhar king...when everyone had been arranged in order upon the mound, the rath was granted to Roalbh'. It can be argued that the poet in the thirteenth century was no better placed than we are to speculate on the function of the place, which was already an ancient monument in his time. But we think again of Fiacc's seventh-century hymn to St Patrick where the poet makes a comparison between the desolate places that were important in pagan times and the bustling metropolises that were the new Christian centres. In this case he specifically associated Emain with former kingship.

Some archaeologists would have been happy to conclude, even without any excavation having taken place, that the mound in Emain Macha may have been used for the inauguration of prehistoric kings. In reviewing the results of the excavation, we have come to the conclusion that the site was to be used for community gatherings and kingly inaugurations. If this is so, what could the internal structure of the mound, particularly the timber building, have symbolised in the context of kingship? We have a large multi-ring structure made of oak posts and beams with a superstructure of some form, probably not a roof in the conventional sense. Large, probably circular, buildings are mentioned in early kingship stories. These are the *bruiden*, the Otherworld hostels, often places of ill omen for kings. There are said to have been five or six royal hostels in Ireland, and, according to the tale *Fled Bricren* ('Bricriu's Feast'), Conchobar had a *bruiden* in Emain Macha. The timber hall had a 'stock' description in the tales, often elaborated with claddings of gold and silver that could not have existed in fact. The structures described may simply represent greatly enlarged houses of Early Christian Ireland, where the tales were recounted and even written. But some aspects of their descriptions suggest that something different from a normal Early Christian period house was imagined. For example, the *bruiden* was consistently described as a 'house of oak', but even high-status Early Christian dwellings were made entirely of woven hazel rods. Normally the only parts made of oak were the door jambs and bed ends.

The classical accounts of the Gauls burning human sacrifices in wooden structures prompted some scholars to see a parallel with the burning of buildings in Irish tales (reminiscent of the 'wickerman' referred to earlier), for example *Togail Bruidne Da Derga*, the 'Burning of Da Derga's Hostel'. The description of the great wooden 'images' on the Continent are reminiscent of the accounts in the early Irish tales of the trapping of warriors in the *bruiden* and the subsequent burning of the buildings. Is there a possibility that the multi-ring timber building in the Navan mound was a model of the ill-fated hostels glimpsed in the later tales? Large wooden structures are mentioned in a number of the Ulster tales, for example Medb's palace at Cruachan, Bricriu's Hostel and Conchobar's *Craebruad* (Red Branch Hall) at Emain Macha. The descriptions all appear to derive from a common prototype. The buildings are of central significance in the tales: they are royal residences or magical 'hostels' where normal relations between this world and the Otherworld are suspended. Given the dates of the written tales that have come down to us, it appears unlikely that this stock description could have any implications for the interpretation of an Iron Age structure uncovered by archaeological excavations: 'Seven ranks there (and) seven compartments (from fire to wall). Frontings of bronze (and) carved work of red yew. Three posts of bronze in the (?) of the house. House of oak with roof of shingles.' There are, however, some similarities between the descriptions of these 'mythical' hostels and the Navan timber structure. It too was very large and round and was made of oak. There were seven spaces between the central post and the outer wall, and there were three parallel aisles. The correspondences between the materials, layout and numbers of elements of the mythic hostel and the Navan structure may be coincidental because in the past the numbers three and seven were commonly magic and may have been enshrined in unrelated ceremonial structures. But the possibility of accidental coincidence must be questioned, since one tale, *Fled Bricren*, also states that a wooden structure of this type existed in Emain Macha/Navan Fort.

According to this story, 'Bricriu's House' was built in the likeness of the *Craebruad* at Emain Macha. The description of Bricriu's house may be taken, therefore, to apply equally to the *Craebruad*: 'A royal apartment for Conchobar was erected at the front of the royal house...round this apartment were built twelve apartments for the twelve warriors of the Ulaid'. Similarly, in *Tochmarc Emire*, 'The Courtship of Emer', Conchobar's palace of the *Craebruad* is described as having 'twelve apartments of the twelve chariot-chiefs around about the king's apartment'. The description of Da Derga's hostel portrays a circular building with a symmetrically subdivided perimeter: '...the road goes through the house. There are seven entrances to the house, and seven apartments between each two entrances. There is only one door, however, and that is placed at the entrance against which the wind is blowing.' Mac Da Thó's hostel is described as 'one of five hostels in Ireland. It had seven doors, seven entrances, seven hearths, seven cauldrons and fifty paces between each pair of doorways.' The size, material, layout and location of the Navan timber structure accord sufficiently well with the stock description of the magical hostel of the literary tradition as to raise the possibility that that the two may be related. In fact Da Derga's hostel was burned with the king inside, the inevitable outcome of a false judgement. It is possible, therefore, that the design of the Iron Age ceremonial building in Navan was based on a mythical prototype. The same myth may have survived to become the stock description of the hostel or king's hall in the Ulster Cycle of tales. It may be significant that the distribution of personages in the mythic hostel of the tales was organised according to a tri-functional pattern (priests/judges, warriors and providers) and was meant to symbolise the proper organisation of a state ruled justly. The mythic hostel is an integral and recurring component of kingship tales. If the wooden structure in the mound was meant to represent such a building, its presence supports the conclusion that the whole purpose of the monument was to create a permanent and respected site for kingship ceremonials.

Conclusion

As one watches a vivid sunset across the wide horizon from the Navan hilltop on a September evening, the whole western sky turns a bright brick-red, throwing the bulk of the ancient mound into a black silhouette. At the same time the moon is low in the sky over the City of Armagh to the east, and the towers of the two venerable cathedrals can be seen dimly lit by the glow of the street lights. As a phenomenon, the continuity of faith in the landscape of Emain Macha from prehistory to the present is similarly remarkable (Fig. 63). Ceremonial monuments of all ages represent humankind's attempts to organise communities along coherent, structured lines and to identify with and become part of the transcendental. As architecture began in attempts to replicate the sacred cosmos, so its beginnings were a necessary stage in people's efforts to understand and interact with the sublime through ritual and science and eventually to reach out to it.

There are two related themes I have been attempting to follow in the course of this little book. One is to discover and explore the varied evidence for past activity in this small area of County Armagh where strange prehistoric earthwork

Fig. 63—View from Haughey's Fort to the medieval cathedral in Armagh with the Navan mound on the right (photo: J. Finegan).

monuments and archaeological finds are so numerous. The other is to grope towards an understanding of what these monuments may have meant to the people who built them. While, for the writer, this may have started as a simple interest in the place where he grew up, the enquiries have involved huge resources and a wide range of experts, some from far afield, who have a shared awareness of the potential interest of this piece of land because of its archaeological and literary heritage.

The significance of the monuments of the Navan Complex is that they contain a representative collection of prestige sites in an area of high economic yield, which was clearly viewed by people in the past as having a special religious significance for at least a millennium from the Middle Bronze Age to the Early Iron Age. Some of the aura of this significance may have come down to us through the literary traditions associated with the place. Since Navan Fort and some of the other late prehistoric sites in Ireland, such as the circular enclosures at Tara and Knockaulin, are probably the last large ceremonial monuments to have been built in prehistoric Europe, they have the potential to lead us into the mind of late prehistory outside the classical world. The wider significance of Navan's archaeology lies in the realm of anthropology, in particular the ingenious ways in which people developed and implemented strategies to survive into the future, economically, institutionally and spiritually, as coherent communities.

Select bibliography

Lincoln, B. 1986 *Myth, cosmos and society: Indo-European themes of creation and destruction*. Cambridge, Massachusetts, and London. Harvard University Press.

Littleton, C.S. 1982 *The new comparative mythology*. Berkeley, Los Angeles and London. University of California Press.

Mac Cana, P. 1970 *Celtic mythology*. London. Hamlyn.

Mallory, J.P. and McNeill, T.E. 1991 *The archaeology of Ulster from colonization to plantation*. Belfast. Institute of Irish Studies.

Mallory, J.P. and Stockman, G. (eds) 1994 *Ulidia: proceedings of the first international conference on the Ulster Cycle of tales*. Belfast and Emain Macha. December Publications.

Newman, C. 1997 *Tara: an archaeological survey*. Dublin. Royal Irish Academy.

Piggott, S. 1975 *The Druids*. London. Thames and Hudson.

Raftery, B. 1997 *Pagan Celtic Ireland*. London. Thames and Hudson.

Rees, A. and Rees, B. 1961 *Celtic heritage*. London. Thames and Hudson.

Ross, A. 1974 *Pagan Celtic Britain*. London. Sphere Books.

Waterman, D.M. 1997 *Excavations at Navan Fort 1961–71* (ed. C.J. Lynn). Belfast. Stationery Office.

Every issue of the journal *Emania*, so far nineteen from 1986 to the present, contains highly relevant material. *Emania* is published by the Navan Research Group, Queen's University, Belfast, and available for purchase from Wordwell, PO Box 69, Bray, Co. Wicklow (tel. +353 1 2765221; fax +353 1 2765207; web www.wordwellbooks.com).